AF646821

Andaman and Nicobar Islands

Green Paradise on the Blue Surface

Attention Authors

Manas Publications is fighting a war to tell the world that India can win the battle not only by bullet but also by pen. We are converting fighters into writers since our country is full of intellectuals but their knowledge is only confined to them. No sincere effort has been made by any publisher to give the right direction to their knowledge and the talent of intellectual is still hidden. An author always gives the raw material in the shape of manuscript and it is the sense of publisher to make it a finished product. We are motivating the intellectuals' mind and publishing their manuscripts for more than two decades and would like to publish your manuscript too. If you or your colleagues have any manuscript or are working on, please don't hesitate to contact us with detailed synopsis and contents for its publication. We take utmost care in production and give a wide publicity to the book and its author. We can also suggest you the title for writing related to your subject, since we are the publishers who believe more in quality than in quantity.

Andaman and Nicobar Islands

Green Paradise on the Blue Surface

Dr. N. Rajavel

Manas Publications
New Delhi-110002 (INDIA)

MANAS PUBLICATIONS
(We Convert Fighters into Writers)
(Publishers, Distributors, Importers & Exporters)
4402/5-A, Ansari Road (Opp. HDFC Bank)
Darya Ganj, New Delhi-110 002 (INDIA)
Off. ✆ 23260783, 23265523, Res. 23842660
Fax: 011-23272766
E-mail: manaspublications@gmail.com
manaspublications@yahoo.com
website: www.manaspublications.in

© Dr N Rajavel

2nd Impression 2014 (FP - 2007)

ISBN: 13 Digits - 978-81-7049-298-6
10 Digits - 81-7049-298-X

₹ 295/-

All rights reserved. This book is sold subject to the condition that it shall not, by way of trade or otherwise, be lent, resold, hired out, or otherwise circulated, without the publisher's prior written consent, in any form of binding, soft cover or e-version etc., except by the authorised companies and without a similar condition including this condition being imposed on the subsequent purchaser and without limiting the rights under copyright reserved above, no part of this publication may be reproduced, stored in or introduced into a retrieval system, or transmitted in any form or by any means (electrical, mechanical, photocopying, recording or otherwise) without prior written permission of the publisher of the book.

Cataloguing/listing of this book for re-sale purpose can be done, only by the authorised companies. Cataloguing/listing or sale by unauthorised distributors/ bookshops/booksellers etc is strictly prohibited and will be legally prosecuted. The views expressed in this book are those of the author and not at all of the publisher.

The publisher is not responsible for the views of the author and authenticity of the data, in any way whatsoever.

All disputes are subject to Delhi jurisdiction only.

Designed at
Manas Publications

Printed in India at
HS Offsets, Delhi and published by Mrs Suman Lata for
Manas Publications, 4402/5-A, Ansari Road,
(Opp. HDFC Bank),
Darya Ganj, New Delhi-110 002 (INDIA)

Preface

I am extremely happy and pleased to place this fatal attraction in the hands of all those who have a love for scenic beauty. Let they be from any part of the world or across the country, their love will bring them to the cool blue surface. This is a clarion call to researchers, students, travel agents, tour operators, industrialists, bankers, entrepreneurs, officers and all those who matter to pack their bags and set sail. This book brings out the beauty, historical importance and fascinations of the A&N Islands.

The ultimate purpose of life is happiness. It is all about lightening and brightening the lives of the living beings and more so in case of human beings. In the real sense, a person living in happiness is the real rich man. A place which gives great happiness and fascination in its entire splendor is certainly called a Paradise or Heaven on Earth. A place laden with natural abundance and which attracts many visitors to view and enjoy its green beauty may also be referred to as Green Paradise. As such the Andaman and Nicobar Islands (A&N Islands) with 86% of its total area covered by its thick green forests has been providing greater happiness to all those who visit these islands. A look at the map shows that Bay of Bengal is part of the eastern segment of the Indian Ocean. The Bay of Bengal looks like a beautiful Blue Surface, which can be enjoyed by the visitors/tourists while travelling by ship. The blue surface has been bearing up the Green Paradise, Andaman and Nicobar Islands.

Fascination is the economic power of drawing people towards the place. The most important resources, from the point of economic development, are the land resources, favourable situation, climate, fertile soil, water resources, fisheries, mineral resources, forest resources, education, socio-cultural resources, historical resources etc. Water resources help in agriculture and plantation; forest resources are of immense value to agriculture and industry. Education plays a very vital role in the process of real human resource development; socio-cultural resources help in the development of moral and discipline etc. The fascinations in the present work are divided into five types, namely informational fascination, historical fascination, social and cultural fascination, educational fascination and places and natural fascinations.

This book covers all aspects of fascinations and attractions of the Andaman and Nicobar Islands in seven chapters. Chapter I is introductory in nature by classifying the tourists from the view point of economics, i.e. economic tourists and non-economic tourists. Chapter II describes the informational fascination. Chapter III deals with the historical fascination. Chapter IV presents the socio-cultural fascinations. Chapter V relates to educational fascination. The places and natural fascinations are given in Chapter VI and Chapter VII provides the conclusion.

This book, written in simple language with the original research work on current problems, will be useful to all lovers of nature.

I thank my children, daughters Raja Sudhaa, Raja Sangeetha and son Raja Velmurugan, for their valuable cooperation and help in putting this book together. I am also indebted to all my friends and well-wishers who extended their help at every stage in completion of this work. I express my sincere thanks to Manas Publications, New Delhi for their cooperation in bringing out the book in record time.

Port Blair **Dr. N. Rajavel**

Contents

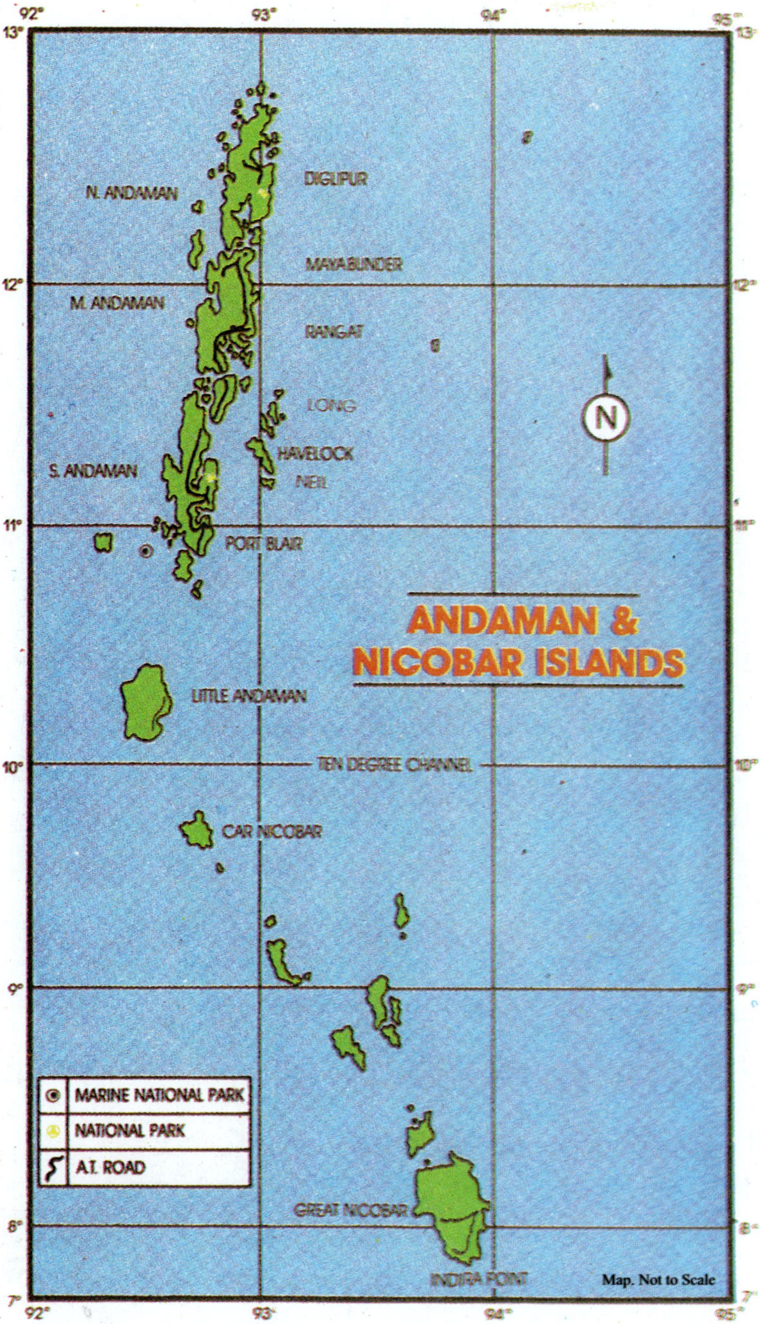

92°
93°
94°
95°
13°
12°
11°
10°
9°
8°
7°
N. ANDAMAN
DIGLIPUR
MAYABUNDER
M. ANDAMAN
RANGAT
LONG
HAVELOCK
S. ANDAMAN
NEIL
PORT BLAIR
N
ANDAMAN &
NICOBAR ISLANDS
LITTLE ANDAMAN
TEN DEGREE CHANNEL
CAR NICOBAR
MARINE NATIONAL PARK
NATIONAL PARK
A.T. ROAD
GREAT NICOBAR
INDIRA POINT
Map. Not to Scale

PORT BLAIR TOWN MAP
CHATHAM
PHOENIX BAY
MINNIE BAY
SERVICES
1 INDIAN AIRLINES
2 SHIPPING CO OF INDIA
3 MARINE & SHIPPING
4 TOURISM OFFICE SECRETARIAT
5 RAJ-NIVAS
6 G.B. PANT HOSPITAL
7 BUS TERMINUS
8 HEAD POST OFFICE
9 TELEGRAPH OFFICE
10 GOVT. COLLEGE
11 ABERDEEN P.S.
12 STATE BANK OF INDIA
13 SYNDICATE BANK
14 CANARA BANK
15 GYMKHANA GROUND
16 TRANSPORT OFFICE
17 FERRY BOOKING/ PHOENIXBAY JETTY
18 STATE LIBRARY
19 GOVT. OF INDIA TOURIST OFFICE
20 HADDO JETTY
21 AIRPORT & TOURIST INFORMATION CENTRE
22 SAGAR TOURS AND TRAVELS
23 SHOMPEN TRAVELS
24 ISLAND TRAVELS
LODGING
25 TOURIST HOME/ MEGAPODE NEST
26 GUEST HOUSE NO. 1
27 CORBYN'S COVE GUEST HOUSE
28 HORNBILL NEST
29 MARINE HILL NOOK NEST
30 MUNICIPAL GUEST HOUSE, D/PUR
31 BAY ISLAND HOTEL
32 ANDAMAN BEACH RESORT
33 SINCLAIRS BAY VIEW
34 N.K. INTERNATIONAL
35 HOTEL DHANALAKSHMI
36 HOTEL SHOMPEN/TRAVELS
37 HOTEL SHALIMAR
38 HOTEL ABHISHEKH
39 HOTEL KAVITHA
40 HOTEL BENGAL K.P.
TOURIST SPOTS
41 CELLULAR JAIL NATIONAL MEMORIAL
42 ANTHROPOLOGICAL MUSEUM
43 FISHERIES MUSEUM
44 CORBYN'S COVE BEACH
45 CHATHAM SAW MILL
46 MINI ZOO
47 MARINA PARK
48 DILTHAMAN TANK
49 COTTAGE INDUSTRIES EMPORIUM
50 ZOOLOGICAL MUSEUM
51 FOREST MUSEUM
Map not to Scale

Busy Port Blair city

Carbines Cave, Port Blair

Dolphin Resort, Havelock

Cinque Island Beach

Jollybouy Island Beach

Friendly Contact with Jarawas: Gifts on the Beach

An Onge Couple

Andaman Water Sports Complex

Shri Vetrimalai Murugan Temple

Seven Wings of the Cellular Jail

Martyer's Memorial at Cellular Jail Compound

Punishment to the freedom fighter

1
Introduction

Paradise

The ultimate purpose of life is to have happiness. It is lightening and brightening the lives of the living beings and more in case of human beings. Happiness is the food of the youth, and delight of the old age. To have a meaningful life, everyone must reach the ultimate purpose of life and goal. Happiness is an intangible but highly valuable asset which is to be created and kept as a reserve as it cannot be purchased from outside for cash. Living happily means living without disease, tension and problems. In real sense, a person living in happiness is the real rich man. A person said to be rich in terms of money and cash without happiness is the poorest person in the real sense of the word. Here, happiness means the quantity of enthusiasm one is having out of his own thinkings and dealings and not at the cost of sufferings of others. Maintaining a happy state of mind means positive thinking in your approach and that is always in your hand. People can reach the state of happiness in two ways. One is through the success of continuous hard work by developing the habits of effectiveness. The other one is visiting an important place which gives full knowledge of its social and cultural aspects, political and historical aspects, educational and economic aspects. The first way of obtaining happiness was limited in nature requiring a lot of special qualities, principles of success and creative vision but this happiness is fully individual-oriented. The second way of getting happiness is by visiting places of great importance which is broad and unlimited in nature. Getting happiness this way includes involving family and friends who together visit places of great importance. The place or places which give great happiness by fascination, enchantment, powerful attraction and charm are, no doubt, said to be Paradise or Heaven on Earth.

Green Paradise

Every human being would prefer heaven and not hell. Heaven means Paradise full of joy, charm and happiness. The place or places with forest resources which attract people from different parts of the world and gives ever-feeling enthusiasm and greater importance and happiness is referred to here as Green Paradise. The Andaman and Nicobar Islands (A&N Islands) with 86% of its total area under green forest and as one of the Union Territories of our country, has been providing great happiness and importance to the people who visit these islands. The A&N Islands are unique in nature and in character to provide happiness to the people. The scenic and natural beauties of these green islands attract people. Different types of people come to these islands as tourists to enjoy Nature's beauty. When most tourists are free from all worries, they spend their days in these islands forgetting all stress.

The Bay of Bengal – A Blue Surface

The Bay of Bengal is part of the eastern segment of the Indian Ocean. Many islands are on the Bay of Bengal Sea. This has commercial importance because of trade contacts between different countries. The maritime region encompassing the countries around the littoral of the Bay always maintained a thriving contact through movement of trade, people, religious, cultural and political missions, which gave the region an autonomous character. The Bay of Bengal looks like a beautiful

Blue Surface, which can be enjoyed by visitors/tourists when they are travelling by ship. The blue surface has been bearing up the Green Paradise Andaman and Nicobar Islands. The Bay of Bengal was a linking factor between the countries bordering it and the cultural and trade links forged by the Bay stretched from China in the East, to West Asia and Africa in the West. The view of China is that it has important interests in the Bay of Bengal region as the connecting link to the Indian Ocean, and the priority given by it to the economic development of Yunan and strategic linkages with Myanmar apparently is in pursuance of its long-term objective of sustaining and strengthening its influence and role in this region.

Habit of Travel

People go from one place to another for various reasons. One cannot claim that he travels aimlessly and with no reason. If one asks a person "why does he travel?", his immediate answer may be the real reason of his travel or atleast he may say "just", "just for pleasure", "to enjoy" etc. That "just" carries a lot of meaning. On one hand, the facilities provided by the employers in the name of leave travel concessions, family compulsions, increase in income, self-interest, cheaper fares, better facilities, provision of cheaper accommodation, celebrations, honeymoons, festivals, historical importance etc. are the main reasons why people visit places. Of all, one important reason is to earn money which is always high on the agenda. On the other hand, the speciality of a particular place will attract people of all kinds from different parts of the country, regions, and the world.

Fascinations

The term "Fascination" means "Power of drawing to oneself". Fascination of a particular place means the power of drawing the people to that place. But the strength of the power, the speed of the power and the retaining capacity of the power, fully depends upon the strength, speed, capacity, and reputation of the place. The resources of the place/country determine the quality of the fascination. If the resources have full economic value, then the pulling power of the fascination will be more and vice versa. The extent of the fascination will pull the entrepreneurs for the exploitations. The attracted entrepreneurs will normally set up the unit with a view to attract the classified people i.e. customers. Such units will carry out all the services to the people who are attracted by travel. Some travel for pleasure, some for education, some for business etc. Whether a particular place is a tourist destination or not will be decided on the basis of the various types of fascinations possessed by the place. A tourist must be satisfied with the fascinations of the destination. An unhappy tourist is like a dangerous turndown friend who will spoil the image of the destination.

Economic Development and Fascination

The economic development of any region is directly related to the attractions and fascinations of the place. Fascination is the economic power of drawing people towards the place. In fact and also in real, the fascination is the motive power of resources to create mobilization of the factors which is the basis for surplus, a determinant of economic growth. It is the proved evidence that the countries with the natural resources have registered a rapid economic development. But at the same time, a country, which has more resources but has no fascination of power, cannot be a rich country. The most important resources, from the point of economic development, are the land resources, favourable situation, climate, fertile soil, water resources, fisheries, mineral resources, forest resources, education, socio-cultural resources, historical resources etc. The situation of the place determines the course and the volume of trade, location of industries etc. Fertility of the soil helps in production and supply of food and raw materials. Water resources help in agriculture and plantation; forest resources are of immense value for agriculture and industry. Education plays a very vital role in the process of real human resource development. Socio-cultural resources help in the development of moral and discipline etc. So, the fascination of a place plays a very vital role in its economic development.

Tourism Fascinations

Tourism has become one of the major source of income and a major factor for economic development and growth in many countries of the world. As already explained, people who go from one place to another are called Tourists and the whole economic activity is called or termed as Tourism. Some people stay in a particular place for a short period, say a day or two, some people may stay for a longer period, say ten days or even for a month. It depends upon the capacity of the fascinations of the place, that is, power of drawing the tourists towards the place. The factors and resources responsible for such power of drawing people are known, in this work, as Tourism Fascinations.

A Green Paradise on the Blue Surface

Andaman and Nicobar Islands is one of the Union Territories of the Union of India. By virtue of its strategic geographical location on the Blue Surface of the Bay of Bengal and rich in Natural Resources, it attracts and receives great attention. By combining the name of the Blue Surface, these islands may be called as "The Bay Islands", once as KALAPANI (the Black water) indicating the dreaded transportation and punishment of the British Government of India. The inhabitants of these islands are scattered far-flung and wide over a distance of 720 Kms. Some of them are found well established in a few towns and innumerable small villages. The towns and small villages have started flourishing only recently because of harbour and airport facilities that have been provided in these islands and slow progress of shipping and other transport facilities. A solid green paradise on the blue surface of Bay of Bengal, Andaman and Nicobar Islands, stretches its long arms of welcome to this paradise.

Andaman and Nicobar Islands – A Place of Fascinations

Andaman and Nicobar Islands is blessed with lot of resources, such as natural resources, forest resources, marine resources, historical resources, socio-cultural resources etc., all such resources have more horse power of fascination and thereby more number of people of different types, that is, tourists are drawn from the different parts of our country and the world. People/Tourists come to these islands for many purposes, namely education and research, to know the history of these islands, to enjoy nature's beauty, to see the socio-cultural life-style of the people of these islands, etc. The Andaman and Nicobar Islands extend its arms and welcomes the tourists of different purposes though its power of fascinations to set up many economic activities for the growth and development. The different types of fascinations are discussed in separate chapters.

Classification of Fascinations

The fascinations can be classified into many types depending upon the available resources and the need of the people who visit the place. But as far as the A&N Islands are concerned, the fascinations are classified into four types, namely Informational fascinations, Social and Cultural fascinations, Educational fascinations and Natural Places fascinations. They are further classified as :

Informational Fascinations

a) Informational Centres

b) Entry/Permissions

c) Dos and Don't

d) Transport (Air and Ship)

e) Procedure to get tickets (Air and Ship)

f) Distance by Road

g) Communication

h) Accommodation

i) Food

j) Tourist Guides

k) Other facilities

Historical Fascinations

a) Andaman and Nicobar Islands
b) Location
c) History
d) Population
e) Groups ot Population
f) Tribals
g) Port Blair City
h) Cellular Jail
i) Freedom Fighters and Those Incarcerated in Cellular Jail

Social and Cultural Fascinations

a) Churches
b) Gurudwaras
c) Mosques
d) Temples
e) Others
f) Cinema Halls
g) Commercial and Industrial Units
h) Educational Institutions
i) Fairs and Festivals
j) Light and Sound Programme
k) Local Life-Style

Educational Fascinations

a) Administrative Set Up
b) Climate
c) Commerce and Industry
d) Economy

e) Education
f) Educational Institutions
g) Geology
h) Growth of Population
i) Resources
j) Socio-Economic Change
k) Topography
l) Tourism
m) Working Population

Places and Natural Fascinations

a) About Ship Journey
b) Beautiful Scenes (Scenic Beauty)
c) Calm and Peaceful Place
d) Climate
e) Duration of Journey
f) Flora and Fauna
g) Light and Sound Programme
h) Places of Interest

A brief description about each fascination is presented in this book delineating the importance of the place.

Tourists/Visitors – A Classification

In the human history during the early past, man has travelled to satisfy his biological needs, whereas during the subsequent periods, he travelled for socio-political, religious and economic purposes. Some travelled for pleasure, some for education, some for business etc., and hence it is very difficult to distinguish and identify the purpose in concrete terms. So practically it is difficult to identify a tourist on the basis of purpose and length of journey. However, on the basis of informal personal contact with tourists

CLASSIFICATION OF FASCINATIONS

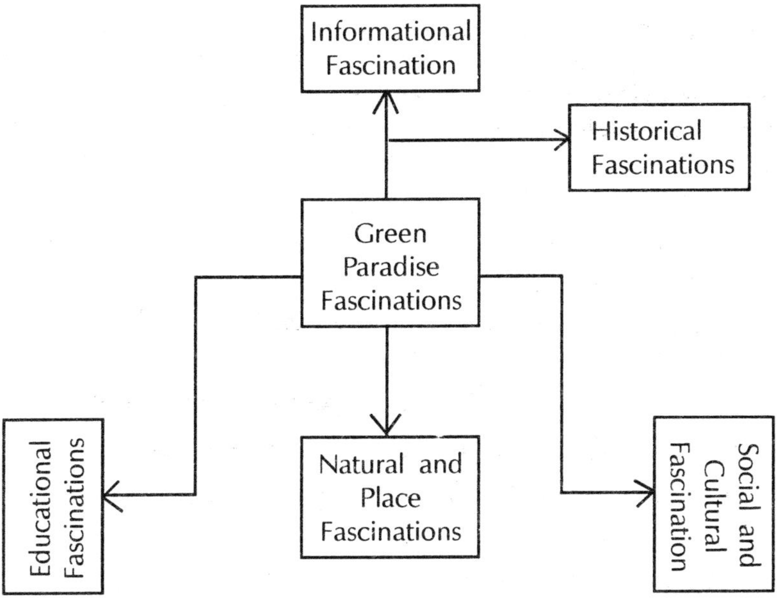

who came to Andaman and Nicobar Islands during the past three years, it has been found that people from many of parts of our country and other countries came here for the following motive :

1. To see all historically important places of these islands
2. To stay and enjoy the natural beauty of these islands
3. To celebrate honeymoon, anniversaries etc.
4. To do research work and other educational purposes
5. To find out business possibilities
6. To know the socio-cultural life of these islands
7. To see the festivals of these islands etc., etc.
8. To stimulate political feelings with politics
9. To organise meetings religiously and regionally
10. To stay as the Govt. guest.
11. To visit this territory as on duty etc., etc.

Hence the tourists or visitors are divided into two major classifications namely Economic Tourists and Non-Economic Tourists. Economic Tourists are those tourists who contribute money for the economic development of these islands. They spend more amounts on stay, food, travel, purchase of goods and services and purchase of some finished products of these islands to the mainland. The following are the characteristics of impact of the arrival of the Economic Tourists:

1. The factors responsible for the growth of tourism will get extra strength.
2. Small business units will be very active in order to satisfy the needs of the tourists.
3. Generally there will be no problem in the places.
4. The number of tourists will always be more.
5. Everybody will be concentrating in his or her own business activities.
6. Government revenue will increase.
7. Unemployment will come down.
8. The service providers will be happy.
9. The per capita income will increase; and in turn
10. The National Income will show a growing trend.

These factors are not only for these islands but for all tourist places. The characteristics of the Economic Tourists are the same, irrespective of the place.

The Non-Economic Tourists are those tourists who do not contribute anything to the economy. Normally they come on government account. The following are the characteristics of the arrival of the Non-Economic Tourists:

1. Lot of disturbances like traffic jam, etc.,
2. Clashes between the regions and religious people, and party people
3. Imbalance of the law and order situation and the allied problems

4. The business units will find difficulty in running their business
5. The service providers will not be happy
6. The number of Non-Economic Tourists is always less
7. The Unemployment problem will be more
8. There will be no increase in the per capita income; and
9. There will be no change in the National Income and sometimes it will be negative also.

All the above reasons are not only for these islands but apply to all tourist places. The characteristics of the Non-Economic Tourists are the same, irrespective of the places. So the tourists are divided as follows under the classified items:

I. Economic Visitors/Tourists

1. Visitors/Tourists for Research and Education
2. Visitors/Tourists for Historical Places
3. Visitors/Tourists for Pleasure
4. Visitors/Tourists for Honeymoon
5. Visitors/Tourists for Anniversaries
6. Visitors/Tourists for Natural Beauty
7. Visitors/Tourists for Religious functions
8. Visitors/Tourists for Socio-Cultural purposes
9. Visitors/Tourists for Business

II. Non-Economic Visitors/Tourists

1. Visitors/Tourists on Government Expenditure
2. Visitors/Tourists as Government Guest
3. Visitors/Tourists for Politics
4. Visitors/Tourists for Preaching Religious Activities

CHARACTERISTICS OF ECONOMIC VISITORS/TOURISTS AND NON-ECONOMIC VISITORS/TOURISTS TO THIS GREEN PARADISE

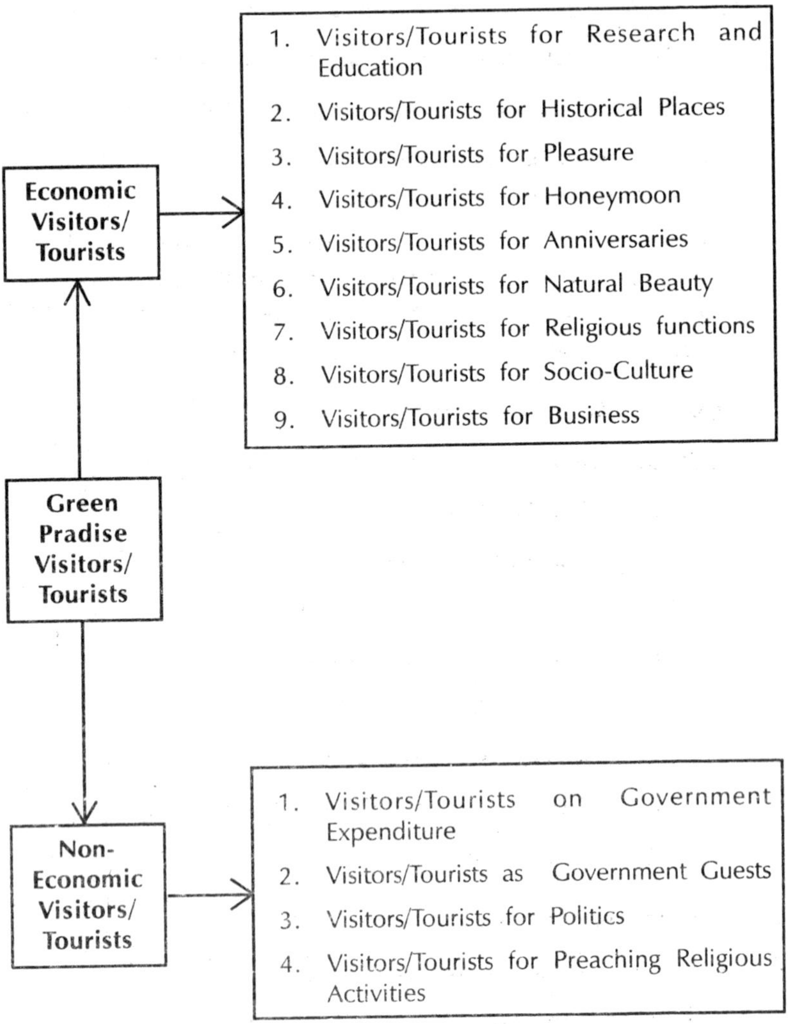

Advantages of Tourism Fascinations

The United Nations declared the year 2002 as International Year of Eco-Tourism. But the importance of this smokeless industry—Tourism—has not been fully realised so far. The contribution of tourism industry to the field of education, trade, commerce and other industry, to job creation, eradication of poverty, increase of the per capita income and economic development as a whole has been largely ignored or underestimated for many years. But now a days, the situation is slightly changing. People have started realising the fact that eco-tourism is the key to sustainable development.

For sustainable development of any country, uninterrupted supply of finance and funds are the basic requirements besides the strong basement of socio-cultural-political environment. Thus social environment, cultural environment and political environment and their growth are the essentials for sustainable development. For all such environments and growth, economic growth is the fundamental factor. Alongwith the economic growth, such environments also grow and prosper this is said to be the Economic Development. If such economic development is advancing and increasing without any symptom of fall, anywhere and at any place, then it is termed as sustainable development. But for economic development, investments are necessary. These investments are made out of savings. The savings are channeled into investments for the economic growth. The income from such investments can only sustain the development. A continuous and uninterrupted flow of income can only sustain the development. For that purpose, investments are to be mobilized or mobilization must take place. This is possible only by the tourism industry. Hence the tourism fascinations are very helpful in the capital mobilization, which is the basis for the economic development.

However, this unique and fascinating wealth of this Green Paradise has not yet been fully realised. The eco-tourism potential of this Paradise provides many opportunities for both the protection of the environment and the development of tourism. Although these islands have a network of parks and national

Although these islands have a network of parks and national parks, the future of this region could be positively changed through the development of eco-tourism.

Of late, Tourism has become one of the most important and fast growing economic sectors of A&N Islands. It has already registered remarkable growth over the last few years with increasing international arrivals. Further challenge is now to develop more eco-tourism products — products that will also be capable of attracting tourists. The unique bio-diversity and rich natural endowment of Andaman and Nicobar Islands provide a big window of opportunity. Hence, the natural beauty of the A&N Islands is very attractive which often urges the writers to term it as the Green Islands in the Marigold Sun, is now being recognised as tourists' paradise by both domestic and foreign tourists.

2

Informational Fascinations

Introduction

Information constitutes the most important part in the package of tourism and travel. This is the prime facility without which the tourists will not get even the first idea about the place, fascinations, etc. Generally, tourists before coming to these far-flung Islands, wish to collect particulars and information regarding the places to see, best season to travel and visit, air tickets, ship tickets, fares, accommodation facilities available, tour operators, items to purchase, how long one can stay etc., accommodation tariff, procedure to get permission, immigration formalities etc. On the whole, some information is to be collected before they come to these Islands in the mainland itself and the rest they can get after reaching these Islands, i.e. in Port Blair.

Information

Information is the basis for all kinds of economic activities. Starting from project work to business work, the information plays a very vital role. Without information, one can't take any decision, one can't plan, one can't organize, one can't control, and one can't communicate and coordinate, budget and report. It is not an exaggeration to say that without information, things may not move in the universe. As already said the fascinations are the base factor for the economic development; informational fascinations are the magnetic inflamed desire and a magnetic allurement about a particular place. Hence, the informational fascinations play an indispensable role in the development of tourism-allied activities in the Andaman and Nicobar Islands.

Green Paradise and Information

Still, and till today, majority of the people of mainland are of the opinion that the Andaman and Nicobar Islands is a very backward area; it is a place of punishment; no facilities are available; it is a place of malaria; big mosquitoes are there; ship to reach these Andaman and Nicobar Islands take more than eight days; the inhabitants (tribals) are very dangerous and they kill the civilians and what not. One more important matter is that, still, some people think that the Andaman and Nicobar Islands is a foreign country. They use stamps of higher value than required while sending letters. During informal talks with tourists, it came to light that there was inadequate information about the transport, how to get in, hotels and accommodation, tours and travels, entertainment facilities etc. Hence the author presents the relevant information about this Green Paradise.

Any person who plans to visit this Green Paradise i.e. Andaman and Nicobar Islands, would like to have all information to plan his tour. Again, he needs information to take a decision regarding the number of days to stay in Andaman and Nicobar Islands. Some tourists, before starting their journey, plan and try to confirm about the various facilities available in the place or destination. As the saying goes, first impression is the best impression, tourist information is counted as the better impression. Whatever be the level of richness in its tourism fascinations, if a destination fails to provide the tourist information, the tourists will not be attracted and will be dissatisfied. A satisfied tourist is the best advertisement but an unhappy tourist is the worst turndown friend. Hence the information about the A&N Islands to the tourists is highlighted in this chapter.

Informational Fascinations

The informational fascinations is divided into the following headings:

- Informational Centres
- Entry/Permissions
- Dos and Don'ts
- Transport (Air and Ship)
- Distance by Road and Sea
- Procedure to get tickets (Air and Ship)
- Communication
- Accommodation
- Food
- Travel agents/Tour operators
- Water Sports
- Swimming Pool
- Other Facilities

Information Centres

Information constitutes the most important part in any tourism package, i.e. Facilities offered to tourists. This is the prime facility without which the tourists will not even get the first idea about the place, attractions, etc. A&N Administration has provided this facility through its own offices both at the mainland and in the Island. Tourism Offices of the Govt. of India in different places and the private travel and tour agents/operators at different parts of our country also share the responsibility of providing necessary information to tourists. For the purpose of information to tourists, the following addresses are given from where all tourists, both domestic and foreign, can obtain various particulars and the necessary information.

INFORMATIONAL FASCINATIONS

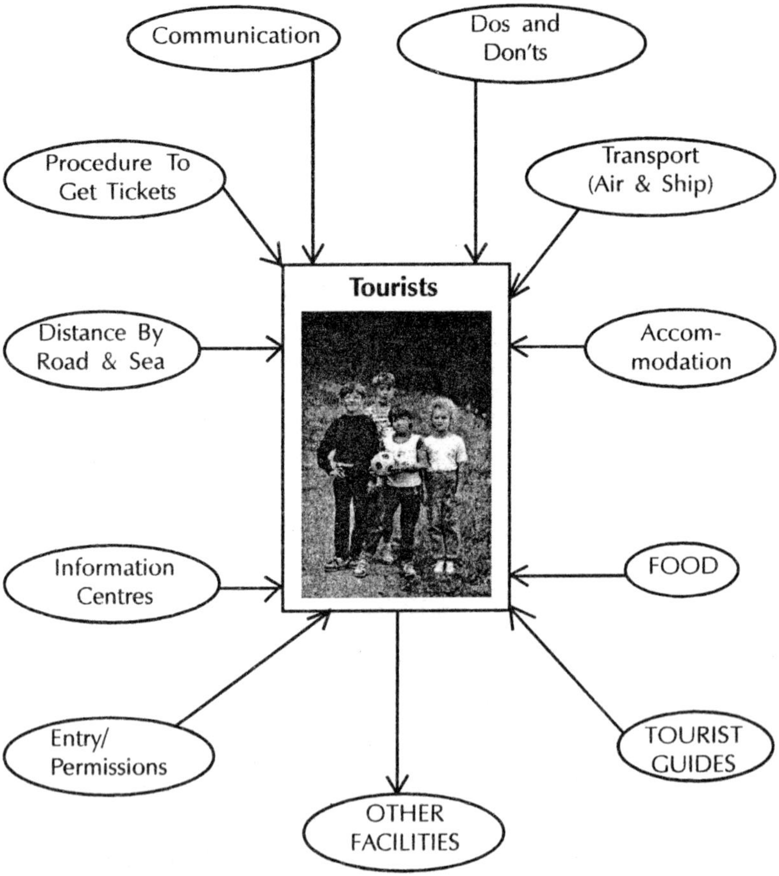

Tourist Information Centres

At Port Blair

		Phone Nos.
1.	Directorate Of I P and T	232694, 232747
2.	Andaman Teal House	234060,234061
3.	Tourist Information Counter (At Veer Savarkar Airport)	232414

4.	Govt. Of India Tourist Office, Junglighat	233006

At New Delhi

1.	Andaman and Nicobar Bhavan 12, Chanakyapuri, New Delhi	26871443 26878120

At Kolkata

1.	Andaman and Nicobar House, 3, A Auckland Place, Kolkata-17	22475084

At Chennai

1.	Andaman House, North Main Road Ext. Anna Nagar West Ext., Padi Village. Chennai	26549294 26549295
2.	ANIIDCO, TTDC Tourism Complex, Walajah Road, Chennai	25360952

How to Get Entry/Permission?

To visit these islands, foreigners require permit and to visit the tribal areas both foreigners and Indians require permit. Andaman and Nicobar Administration is very strict as far as the necessity of entry/permission is concerned. Some agents are seeding the interest of open-ness in the minds of tourists to visit the tribal areas. But after coming to Port Blair, they get upset and are disappointed when they come to know that they have to take permission to go to the tribal areas. This disappointment and frustration etc. are due to lack of information about the rules and regulations of entry, permission etc. Therefore, it is necessary to clear the misrepresentation, made by some writers without having properly studied the rules and regulations related to visit these areas so that no tourist feels misled about these Islands. No doubt, the tourism industry is accelerated in these Islands but at the same time, due to some technical and security reasons all the Islands under this territory are not open to tourists, including the Indian tourists. As far as the entry formalities are concerned, at present, the following position is in force as per the information from the Directorate of Information Publicity and Tourism, Andaman and Nicobar Islands, Port Blair.

Foreigners

Foreigners can obtain the entry/permission immediately on the arrival at Port Blair either by flight or by ship from the authorities for 30 days which can further be extended for another 15 days. Foreign tourists can stay in these Islands (permitted areas) initially for a period of 30 days. However, with the permission of the Govt. of India, the Foreign tourists can stay for more than 30 days also. For the purpose of the 30 days stay, they require a permit which is to be (but can be easily) obtained from the immigration authorities on the arrival at Port Blair either at the airport or at the harbour. The Foreign tourists can also obtain the permit from the Indian Embassy in their respective country itself or from any of the 4 Foreigners' Regional Registration Office (FRRO) situated in Chennai, Kolkata, Mumbai and Delhi. Their mailing addresses are as follows:

1. **Chennai**
   The Officer In charge
   Foreign Regional Registrar Office (FRRO)
   9, Village Road
   Chennai. Phone: (044) 2478210.

2. **Kolkata**
   The Officer In-charge
   FRRO, 237, A.J.Bose Road
   Kolkata
   Phone: (033) 2443301.

3. **Mumbai**
   The Officer In-charge
   FRRO, Special Branch II Annexe 2,
   Office of the Commissioner of Police,
   Dadabhoy Navaroji Road,
   Mumbai
   Phone (022) 2268111.

4. Delhi
The Officer In-charge
FRRO,
Ist Floor, Hans Bhawan,
Tilak Bridge
Delhi
Phone (011) 2272790

Night Halt

The places covered by this permit for night halt are:

1. South Andaman Islands,
2. Middle and North Andaman Islands,
3. Little Andaman Islands (Except the tribal reserve areas)
4. Neil Island,
5. Havelock Island,
6. Long Island,
7. Diglipur,
8. Baratang Island,
9. North Passage Island, and
10. Islands in the Mahatma Gandhi Marine National Park (excluding Twin, Tarmugli, Malay, and Pluto islands),
11. Night halt in the Marine National Park, with permission only.

Areas Open to Tourists

Areas where the tribals Jarawa and Sentinalese are living are completely prohibited for all tourists including Indian tourists. The places/islands where Onges, Great Andamanese are living and places/islands where Nicobar tribals are living are also designated as restricted areas. However, only Indian tourists are granted permission by the A&N Administration to visit these restricted areas and no foreign tourist is granted permission to visit any of the tribal areas. During the early years, the foreigners were not allowed to visit and stay beyond the municipal limits of Port Blair. Later, the Government allowed foreigners to visit Jolly Buoy Islands, Redskin Islands, Wandoor National Park, and Cinque Islands during day time only. Ross Island, South Cinque Island, Narcondum Island, Interview Island, Brother Island, Sister Island and Barren Island can be visited on board vessels only. But now, besides the above places/Islands, the following places/ areas/Islands have also been declared open by the Govt. of India to foreign tourists:

1. Havelock Island in South Andaman
2. Mount Harriet in South Andaman
3. Neil Island in South Andaman
4. Rangat in Middle Andaman
5. Mayabunder in Middle Andaman
6. Long Islands in Middle Andaman, and
7. Diglipur Islands in North Andaman

Indian nationals need no permit to visit Andaman and Nicobar Islands. However, visiting tribal areas of Andaman and Nicobar District is prohibited. Permits to visit the tribal areas can be granted by the Deputy Commissioner, Andaman District, Port Blair.

Dos And Don'ts

All tourists are expected that they should not damage the tourism resources particularly the marine life resources. For that purpose, the A&N Administration has given the following guidelines in the form of Dos and Don'ts.

Dos

* Treat the Park with respect as it is a sanctum sanctorum of our precious natural heritage.
* Make use of the services of tourist guides.
* Learn more about coral reefs, other marine life and tropical forests. This will make your visit more enjoyable.

* Help us to keep the Park clean. Always bring back litter.
* Take care of the reef, not just for yourself but for all who will follow.
* Give your valuable comments and observations for ensuring better park management.

Don'ts

* Do not enter the Park without permit.
* Do not collect, destroy or remove any living or dead animal/plant.
* Do not collect dead coral or break live coral. Please do not stand on the coral reef while snorkeling.
* Do not take videos or films without permit.

Transport

Tourism and transport are inter-related with one another. Tourism will improve if transport facilities are good and transport will improve if tourism is good and hence they are inseparable. Transport and communication are considered as an integral part of tourism. In the words of Robinson, "Transport had been at one time a cause and an effect of growth of tourism. Improved transport facility has stimulated tourism; the expansion of tourism has stimulated transport".

Tourism in Andaman and Nicobar Islands is of a special type. Foreign tourists first come to Delhi or Mumbai or Chennai or Kolkata and from there they should reach Kolkata, Chennai or Vishakhapatnam. After reaching any one of the three cities they have to wait for a ship or a flight to Andaman and Nicobar Islands (Port Blair). After arriving at Port Blair, tourists go to different places in Andaman and Nicobar Islands. The Indian tourists come to Port Blair from Chennai, Kolkata or Vishakhapatnam. The transport facility available in or provided by A&N Islands is classified, for the purpose of the present work, into two categories namely:

1. Islands-Mainland Transport, and 2. Inter-Island Transport

Islands-Mainland Transport

Under this category, both flights and ships are utilised. This sector of the transport forms an integral part of the Island tourism. Tourists—both Indian and foreign—come to these islands only by means of flight and ships which are considered to be the only transport system of these Islands with the mainland of India. Both the modes of transport, shipping service and air service are considered equally important. All items from cement to sugar, vegetable to salt are brought into these islands both by ships and flights—more by the ships. Hence Island-Mainland transport consists of:

A. Shipping Service, and B. Air Service

Shipping Service

Regular passenger ship services are available to Port Blair from Chennai, Kolkata and Vishakhapatnam and back. There are three to four sailings every month from Kolkata and Chennai to Port Blair and vice versa. There is one sailing from Vishakhapatnam in a month. The voyage takes about 50 to 60 hours.

The number of ships available for tourists and passengers, on an average, is minimum 2 and maximum is 2-3. Ships are operated on Port Blair-Chennai-Port Blair sector for a minimum of 4 times and on Port Blair-Kolkata-Port Blair sector for a minimum of 3-4 times in a month. The tourists—both domestic and foreign—can get their reservation of tickets, shipping programmes and other relevant information from the tour cities, namely Mumbai, Kolkata, Chennai and Vishakhapatnam of Mainland of India itself. Normally, the shipping programmes are made by the A&N Administration and sent to these places for use of the tourists. The following addresses are very useful to tourists for all the necessary information:

a) Shipping Corporation of India Ltd.
Apeejay House, 4th Floor,
Dinsnaw Wacha Road, Mumbai - 400 020
Tel: 22822101/22823316 Fax: (022) 22022438

b) Shipping Corporation of India Ltd.
Shipping House, No. 13, Strand Road, Kolkata - 700 001
Tel: 22482354, 22488013
Fax: (033) 22482035, 22480377

c) Shipping Corporation of India Ltd.
Jawahar Building, Rajaji Salai,
Chennai - 600 001
Tel: (044) 25231401, Fax: (044) 25231218

d) Shipping Corporation of India Ltd.
Aberdeen Bazar, Port Blair - 744101
Tel: (03192) 233347, 233590
Fax: (03192) 233778

e) The Deputy Director of Shipping Services,
A&N Administration, 6, Rajaji Salai,
Chennai - 600 001
Tel: (044) 25220841/25226873

f) The Director of Shipping Services
A&N Administration,
Phoenix Bay Jetty, Port Blair
(For MV Nancowry and MV Swarajdweep)
Tel: (03192) 232528/232742
Fax: (03192) 230480

g) M/s A.V. Bahanojirow and Garuda
Pattabhiramayya and Co.,
Post Box No. 17, Vishakhapatnam
(Agent - Shipping Corporation of India Ltd.)
Tel: (0891) 2565597/2562661,
Fax: 2566507/2549224

Shipping schedules are also available at the websites www.andaman.nic.in and www.and.nic.in

Duration of Journey

As per official statistics the ships are expected to reach the destination within 54 hours, but practically the ship journey takes and consumes 3 nights and 2 days or 3 days and 2 nights depending upon the weather conditions adverse and/or favourable. If weather conditions are favourable, the ship reaches the destination even before the scheduled time, otherwise it takes even more than 5 days. But during the tourist season, ships reach destinations as per the scheduled time.

Air Transport

Next to shipping service, air service is considered to be second lifeline of these Islands. Though the air transport is one of the means of travel, here in these Islands, the air service is considered as an essential one and is utilized for quick travel. Air transport service to these islands is provided by two autonomous organisations, namely the Indian Airlines and Jet Airways. Though the air transport is generally viewed as a luxurious means of travel, it is considered as one of the essential means of transport to this Green Paradise. It significantly contributes to the development of tourism in this lush green heaven. The air traffic to and from this Island is divided into two sectors, namely:

1. Chennai-Port Blair-Kolkata
2. Kolkata-Port Blair-Chennai

For all these sectors Indian Airlines has been doing a fairly good service in transportation of the tourists to and from this territory through its subsidiary company Alliance Airways w.e.f November 1996, and before that the Indian Airlines itself was doing the service. The Jet Airways also joined in the Air Transport service w.e.f 1998 onwards. Generally, the air journey is quick and pleasant, though it is comparatively expensive. But people of this territory use the air service as the only means to go to the mainland and back on urgent occasions. The duration of journey is about 2 hrs. The tourists can approach any of the Indian Airlines or Jet Airways Offices in any country for reservation, information and tickets etc.

Inter-Island Transport

Inter-Island Transport system is the internal nervous system of the A&N Islands. This transport system connects all the inhabited islands of this territory. As these islands are located at a considerable distance from each other. All produces and products of these islands are distributed among them through the network system of Inter-Island transport. This network system consists of two kinds of transport, namely water transport and road transport.

Inter-Island Water Ways

The capital of A&N Islands, Port Blair is connected with other Islands through the water and road transport. The Inter-Island water transport is further divided into Inter-Island ship service and foreshore ferry service. The Inter-Island water transport connects the different and distant islands with one another. Four passenger-cum-cargo ships are plying between the Islands. Infact these ships are the backbone of Inter-Island Transport. These ships are under the Operational control of Director of Shipping Services. These ships may voyage from Port Blair to Diglipur in North and Campbell Bay in South. A round voyage from Port Blair to Diglipur takes three days and from Port Blair to Campbell Bay seven days. While making voyage these vessels touch the different Islands namely Hut Bay, Nancowry, Car Nicobar, Rangat, Mayabunder, Neil, Havelock etc.

Foreshore Ferry Service

This type of Inter-Island Water Service is operated by the A&N Administration between Port Blair and near by Islands and Ports like Neil, Havelock, Rangat, Kadamtala, Baratang etc. The distance by sea from Port Blair to important places of A&N Islands in kms. is given in tables below:

Table : 2.1
Distance by Sea from Port Blair

From	To	Distance (in km)
Port Blair	Diglipur	183
	Mayabunder	155
	Rangat	92
	Long Island	84
	Havelock	38
	Oral Katcha	64
	Wrefter	49
	Long Island (via Oral Katcha)	82
	Mayabunder via Havelock	137
	Mayabunder via Long Island	135
	Little Andaman	121
	Car Nicobar	274
	Narcondum	256
	Nancowry	429
	Nancowry via Car Nicobar	420
	Barren Island	137
	Neil Island	37
	Baratang	64
	Kadamtala	92
	(Uttara Jetty)East Island	219
	Katchal	416
	Campbell Bay	537
	South Bay (Great Nicobar)	548

Source : Basic Statistics, A&N Administration, Port Blair

Table : 2.2
Distance by Sea between Important Places

From	To	Distance (in km)
Car Nicobar	Chowra	100
	Teressa	82
	Katchal	146
	Nancowry	150
	Campbell Bay	83
Nancowry	WB Katchal	91
	Kandul	37
	Pulomilo	27
Narcondum	East Island	137
	Diglipur	13
	Mayabunder	155
	North Sentinel	361
	Hut Bay	365

Source : Basic Statistics, A&N Administration, Port Blair

Table : 2.3
Distance by Sea between Important Places

From	To	Distance (in km)
Terressa	Nancowry	55
Campbell Bay	Kondul	55
Bareen Island	Mayabunder	121
	Long Island	100
	Nancowry	465
Kondul	Pulomilo	37

Source : Basic Statistics, A&N Administration, Port Blair

Road Transport

The roads are the main means of travel in a particular island. Rail transport is totally absent in these islands and hence road transport is very important for both long and short distance. Road transport in each island of this territory has brought a significant change in the tourism industry and other allied activities. Road transport gives opportunity to tourists to enjoy the places, forests, nallahs etc. from close quarters. Now one can travel by bus even upto Diglipur. Whenever the bus stops at important places, one understands the way of living of the local people, local conditions, cultural style, social movement etc. Distance by road between the places is given in Table 2.4.

Table : 2.4
Distance by Road from Port Blair Bus Terminus

From	To	Distance (in km)
Port Blair Bus Terminus	Chatham	5
	Haddo Jetty	5
	Buniyada Bad	5
	Dairy Farm	5
	Shadipur	5
	Dolly Gunj	10
	Bird Line	12
	School Line	6
	Garacharma	10
	Teylarebad	12
	Calicut	14
	Sippighat	14
	Minnie Bay	10
	Pema Tekkri	16
	Chouldhari	20
	Burma Nala	20

(Contd.)

From	To	Distance (in km)
Port Blair Bus Terminus	Manjeri	24
	Port Mout	24
	Madhuban	75
	Carbynscove	7
	Mount Harriet	55
	Namunaghar	30
	Chidia Toppu	28
	Wandoor	30
	Tirur	36
	Dandas Point	32
	Ferrargunj	34
	Wimberlygunj	42
	Jirkatang	64
	Bambooflat Jetty	46
	Middle Strait	100
	Rangat	170
	Mayabunder	240

Source : Basic Statistics, A&N Administration.

So, each means of transport in these islands has its own significant role. Though the length of roads is less in these islands the longest road called Andaman Trunk Road (ATR) connects a number of villages and places of tourist interest. The number of private buses and govt. buses plying on the roads of A&N Islands has been increasing. The tourism department organises sight-seeing programmes on road by their own buses and vans. Likewise, some private lodge owners also have their own buses and help the tourists who stay in their lodges/hotels. Some tourists, invited by their friends and relatives stay with them and use their scooters, motorcycles or even cars for sight seeing purposes. Recent, a few entrepreneurs have started a new facility for the tourists of these Islands, i.e. giving scooter, scooty, motorcycle, TVS50, M-80 etc., to tourists on hire basis.

Procedure to Get Tickets

The tourists have to come to Chennai, Viṣhakhapatnam or Kolkata at least two days in advance if they have already spoken to officials of the above addressed offices or reserved their tickets, otherwise atleast five days in advance and contact the officials of the above offices or the ticket issuing authority in order to purchase tickets. The prescribed application form is to be filled up and two passport size photographs per head/per ticket are also to be attached. The tickets are issued on first-come-first serve basis. The tourists are advised to contact the offices at least 15 days before by telegram/fax/post or through telephone.

Communication

In A&N Islands, the Port Blair city has a well-developed network of modern means of communication like Speed Post, Telegram, Telephone, Cell, STD/ISD facility, Fax, Tele-printer, Modern Wireless, Inter-Island Telecommunication facilities etc. But those islands and places that are far away from the city, of course, lack many of the communication facilities but are well-connected with wireless system. The Port Blair city has one Head Post Office, one Head Telegraph Office and one Telephone Exchange.

Besides the telecommunication facilities, which are considered to be one of the basic facilities to the tourism industry, books and magazines, cinema, feature films, televisions, All India Radio are the other moulding instruments, as far as communication facilities are concerned with tourism industry. The A&N Islands have been provided with television (Doordarshan) and All India Radio facilities. Port Blair Doordarshan and Port Blair All India Radio, having their studios at Delanipur (two kms. from the Port Blair bus terminus) have been providing an excellent means of transforming the ideas to the most interior parts where no other means of communication is possible.

Accommodation

A visitor/tourist cannot, generally, have any known person in a new place. So he expects safe accommodation at a nominal tariff in accessible area. Hence the accommodation plays a vital role in the promotion of tourism in these Marigold Islands. The present situation regarding the accommodation is excellent. The available tourist-accommodation facility in A&N Islands is given below:

Table : 2.5
Accommodation at Port Blair

Hotels and Beds		No.
No. of Hotels	:	45
No of Beds	:	1705
No. of Govt. Guest Houses	:	5
No. of Beds in Guest Houses	:	200

Source : Tourism Department, A&N Admn. Port Blair

Details of Accommodation

The details of accommodation provided by different sectors are given in the following tables. Names of the guest houses, circuit houses, lodges, etc., and the number of the beds available in each type of accommodation are given in the tables.

Table : 2.6
Accomodation in the Govt. Sector

Sl.No.	Name of the Guest House	No. of Beds
1.	Andaman Teal House, Port Blair	60
2.	Circuit House, Haddo, Port Blair	40
3.	Circuit House, South Point, Port Blair	80
4.	Circuit House, Marine Hill	12
5.	Circuit House, Corbyn's Cove	8
	Total	200

Table : 2.7
Accommodation in PSU and Municipal GH
PUBLIC SECTOR UNDERTAKING

Sl.No.	Name of the Hotel	No. of Beds
1.	Megapode Nest (under lease from Tourism department)	56

MUNICIPAL GUEST HOUSE

Sl.No.	Name of the Hotel	No. of Beds
1.	Aberdeen Guest House	49
2.	Yatri Niwas	42

Table : 2.8
Accommodation in Private Sector

Sl.No.	Name of the Hotel	No. of Beds
1.	Abhshiek	85
2.	Acc	37
3.	Anand Lodge	18
4.	Andaman Tourist Cottage	74
5.	Atithi Palace	16
6.	Atlanta Cottage	16
7.	Azad Lodge	13
8.	Bengal Kp	51
9.	Blair	50
10.	Central Lodge	24
11.	Comfort Inn	14
12.	Dhanalakshmi	100
13.	Fortune Resort Bay Island	90
14.	Gem Continental	18
15.	Golden Beach Resort	58
16.	Heritage Home International	30

(Contd.)

Sl.No.	Name of the Hotel	No. of Beds
17.	Holiday Inn	16
18.	Holiday Resort	32
19.	Hornbill Nest Resort (Under Lease From Tourism Dept.)	50
20.	Jagannath Guest House	24
21.	Jai Mathi	24
22.	Janata Guest House	24
23.	Kavitha	44
24.	Maya Raj	16
25.	Msm Hotel	31
26.	Nagri Inn	16
27.	Nair Service Society Cottages	6
28.	NK International	60
29.	Paradise Inn	16
30.	Peerless Beach Resort	102
31.	Phoenix Lodge	16
32.	Ram Niwas	68
33.	Sagar Alok Lodge	24
34.	Sampat Lodge	36
35.	Sea View Nest	21
36.	Sentinel	50
37.	Shah N' Shah	38
38.	Shalimar	30
39.	Shompen	90
40.	Sinclairs	52
41.	Sky Lodge	16
42.	Swagat Lodge	21
43.	Tourist Nest	13
44.	Andaman Teal House	60
45.	Palika Palace	29
46.	T.S.G. Emerald View	38
	Total	1727

ACCOMODATION OUTSIDE PORT BLAIR

Table : 2.9
Accommodation In South Andaman (Rural)
(Govt. Accommodations)

Sl.No.	Name of the Guest House	Maintained By
1.	Forest Rest House Wandoor	Forest Dept.
2.	Forest Rest House, Chidyatapu	Forest Dept.
3.	Forest Rest House, Mount Harriet	Forest Dept.
4.	Guest House, Ferrargunj	APWD
5.	Guest House, Wright Myo	APWD

Private

Sl.No.	Name of the Hotel	No. of Beds
1.	Palm Grove Eco-Resort, Prothrapore	20
2.	Mangrove Bay resort, Wandoot	12

Table : 2.10
Accommodation in Baratang Island

Sl.No.	Name of the Guest House	Maintained By
1.	Forest Rest House, Nilambur	Forest Dept.
2.	Inspection Bungalow	APWD
3.	Panchayat Guest House	Panchayat

Table : 2.11
Kadamtala

Sl.No.	Name of the Guest House	Maintained By
1.	Govt. Guest House	APWD

Table : 2.12

Accommodation in Rangat (Govt. Accommodation)

Sl.No.	Name of the Guest House	Maintained By
1.	Hawksbill Nest, Curt Bert Bay	Dte. of I P and T
2.	Guest House, Rangat	APWD
3.	Rest House, Betapur	APWD
4.	Guest House, Bakultala	Forest Dept.

Private

Sl.No.	Name of the Guest House	No. of Beds
1.	AVIS	10
2.	DREAM	16

Table : 2.13

Accommodation in Diplipur (Govt. Accommodation)

Sl.No.	Name of the Guest House	Maintained By
1.	Guest House	APWD

Public Sector Undertaking — ANIFPDC

Sl.No.	Name of the Hotel	No. of Beds
1.	ANIFPDC Guest House	4
2.	Ray Hill Resort	8

Private

Sl.No.	Name of the Hotel	No. of Beds
1.	S and S Lodge	15
2.	Swiflet Nest, Karmatang (under lease from Tourism dept.)	24

Table : 2.14

Accommodation in Diplipur (Govt. Accommodation)

Sl.No.	Name of the Guest House	Maintained By
1.	Turtle Resort, Kalipur	Dte. of I P and T
2.	Rest House, Diglpur	APWD
3.	Rest House Ariel Bay Jetty	APWD
4.	NHPC Guest House, Kalara	NHPC
5.	Rest House, Kalighat	APWD
6.	Rest House, Kishori Nagar	APWD
7.	Guest House, Ariel Bay	Forest Dept.

Table : 2.15

Accommodation in Neil Island (Govt. Accommodation)

Sl.No.	Name of the Guest House	Maintained By
1.	Hawabill Nest	Dte. of I P and T
2.	Guest House	APWD

PRIVATE

Sl.No.	Name of the Guest House	No. of Beds
1.	Cocon Huts	20
2.	Pearl park	12

Table : 2.16

Accommodation in Rangat (Govt. Accommodation)

Sl.No.	Name of the Guest House	Maintained By
1.	Dolphin Yatri Niwas	Dte. of I P and T
2.	Guest House	APWD

Accommodation in Havelock (Govt. Accommodation)

Sl.No.	Name of the Guest House	No. of Beds
1.	Jungle Resort	36
2.	Wild Orchid	16
3.	MS Guest House	22
4.	Sea View	14

Private

Table : 2.17

Accommodation in Long Island (Govt. Accommodation)

Sl.No.	Name of the Guest House	No. of Beds
1.	Forest Rest House	6

Table : 2.18

Accommodation in Little Andaman (Govt. Accommodation)

Sl.No.	Name of the Guest House	No. of Beds
1.	APWD Guest House	12

Public Sector Undertaking – ANIFPDC

Sl.No.	Name of the Guest House	No. of Beds
1.	Guest House	4
2.	Beach Resort, Buttler Bay	19

Food

Food is one of the vital factors which determine the growth and development of tourism industry. Tourist destination should have the food facilities suitable for all kinds of tourists. What is a suitable food to Bengali tourists may not be suitable to Tamil tourists and Malayali tourists and so is the case with foreign tourists too. As far as food is concerned, all accommodations/hotels provide limited types of food. Indian style and foreign style are also available in all hotels and restaurants. Tourists can enjoy the food fully with prior intimation/reservation. The restaurants and their addresses are given below.

Table : 2.19
List of Restaurants at Port Blair

Sl. No.	Name of the Restaurant	Type of Food Served*	Whether Bar Attached*
1.	Amigos	South Indian/North Indian/ Chinese/Continental	No
2.	Ananda	South Indian/North Indian/ Chinese	No
3.	Anapurna	South Indian/North Indian/ Chinese	No
4.	Badshah	South Indian/North Indian/Chinese	No
5.	Corbyns Delight (Peerles Resort)	South Indian/North Indian/ Chinese/Continental	Yes
6.	Daawath	South Indian/North Indian	Yes
7.	Delhi Restaurant	South Indian/North Indian/Chinese	No
8.	Dhanalakshmi	South Indian/North Indian/Chinese	No
9.	Gagan	South Indian/North Indian/Chinese	No
10.	Gem Continental	North Indian/ Chinese/Continental	Yes
11.	Hotel ACC	South Indian/North Indian/Chinese	No
12.	Hotel M.S.M	North Indian/ Chinese/Continental	Yes
13.	Hotel Milan	South Indian/North Indian	No
14.	Jaimathi	South Indian	Yes
15.	Kattaboman	South Indian	No
16.	Light House Restaurant	South Indian/North Indian/Chinese	Yes
17.	Maharaja	South Indian/North Indian/Chinese	Yes
18.	Majestic	South Indian/North Indian	No
19.	Mandalay (Fortune Resort bay island)	South Indian/North Indian/ Chinese/Continental	Yes
20.	Megapode Nest	South Indian/North Indian/ Chinese/Continental	Yes
21.	National	South Indian/North Indian/Chinese	No

(Contd.)

Sl. No.	Name of the Restaurant	Type of Food Served*	Whether Bar Attached*
22.	Roof Top Restaurant and Zebra Bar (Shompen)	South Indian/North Indian/ Chinese/Continental	Yes
23.	Shalimar	South Indian/North Indian/Chinese	Yes
24.	Tillai	South Indian/North Indian/ Chinese/Continental	No
25.	Udupi	South Indian/North Indian	No
26.	Vishranti	South Indian/North Indian/Chinese	Yes
27.	Waves (under lease from Tourism Department)	South Indian/North Indian/ Chinese/Continental	Yes

* **Source :** Tourism Dept. A&N Admn., Port Blair, — At the time of Data Collection

Travel Agents/Tour Operators

Generally the tourist attractions, entry facilities, transport facilities, accommodations etc. are the essential factors of the tourism industry and particularly in A&N Islands. But all these factors are independent and hence they are to be coordinated. So an intermediary agency is required to function as a coordinator who is termed as travel agents. Normally, they as tour operators have all transport facilities, information and guides etc. with them at different points in order to facilitate the tourists to reach the destination, place of interest etc. Their role in tourism industry is immense and they provide a number of attractive incentives to the tourists. The travel agents are divided into three categories namely, International Level Agents, National Level Agents and Regional Level Agents. As far as these islands are concerned, the travel agents are confined to the regional level. However, one or two agents do have some connections with the Kolkata/Chennai agents who are also the regional agents. The list of travel agents or tour, boat and scuba diving operators in these islands is given below:

Table : 2.20
Travel Agents/Tour Operator

1.	A&N Islands Tours and Travels	Vehicle on hire
2.	Aloka World Travels	Vehicle on hire
3.	Andaman & Nicobar Tours & Travels	Vehicle on hire, Air Tickets
4.	ANIIDCO	Package Tour , Air Tickets
5.	Chitir Travels	Air Ticket
6.	Darshan Tours and Travels	Package Tour, Vehicle on hire
7.	Deep Tour and Travel	Vehicle on hire
8.	Gem Tour and Travels	Vehicle on hire
9.	Gurunanak Travels	Package Tours, Vehicle on hire
10.	Hindustan Tours and Travels	Vehicle on hire, Air Tickets
11.	Island Travel	Package Tour, Air Tickets
12.	Kathay Travel aids	Vehicle on hire, Package tour
13.	Lokenath Travel	Vehicle on hire, Package tour
14.	MSM Tours	Vehicle on hire
15.	Modern Tours and Travels	Vehicle on hire, Package tour
16.	Mother India Travels	Vehicle on hire, , Package tour
17.	Naba Tours and Travels	Vehicle on hire
18.	Prashant Travels	Two-wheeler on hire
19.	Ritika Travels	Vehicle on hire
20.	S.R. Travels, Haddo	Vehicle on hire, Air Tickets
21.	Sagar Tours and Travels, PVT Ltd.	Package Tours
22.	Shiva Laxmi Tours and Travels Agency	Vehicle on hire
23.	Shompen Travels	Package Tours, Air Tickets
24.	St. Jude Travels & Tours, Goal Ghar	Air tickets
25.	T.S.G. Tour wings	Package Tours, two-wheeler on hire
26.	T.S.G. Travels	Vehicle on hire, Air Tickets
27.	Tasneem Tours and Travels	Package Tours, Vehicle on hire
28.	Travel World	Package Tours, Vehicle on hire, Air Tickets
29.	Galaxy Tours and Travels	Vehicle on hire
30.	G. S. Tours and Travels	Vehicle on hire
31.	Shiv Shakti Tour and Travels	Vehicle on hire

Table : 2.21
Boat Operators

1.	Bay Watch Tours and Travels	Boats on hire
2.	Island Water Sports	Boats on hire and water sports
3.	Shompen Travels	Boats on hire
4.	S.R Travels	Boats on hire
5.	Speed Motors Travels	Boats on hire

Table : 2.22
Scuba Diving Operators

1.	Andaman Scuba Club	Scuba Diving operator
2.	Andaman Divers Pvt. Ltd.	Scuba Diving Operator
3.	Laccadives	Scuba Diving Operator
4.	Samudrika	Scuba Diving Operator

They organise tours regularly as the tourism department is doing. The tour consists of (1) City Tour which covers Cellular Jail, Mini Zoo, Cottage Emporium, Anthropological Museum, Samundrica, Chatham Saw Mill, Gandhi Park, Marina Park, etc. (2) Carbyn's Cove Tour which covers only Carbyn's Cove beach. (3) Chidiatoppu Tour which covers only Chidiyatappu. (4) Excursion around South Andaman which includes Mahatma Gandhi National Marine Park, Wandoor, Red Skin, Jolly Bouy, Wandoor Beach etc. (5) Rose Islands Tour which covers only Rose Island. Besides these tours, there is one more tour named Viper Harbour Cruise Tour which includes around five jetties.

Water Sports

In A&N Islands, there is no river which can provide boating facility to the tourists. But for the purpose of boating there are water sports complexes available in Port Blair city. Shippighat Water Sports Complex, Gandhi Park Water Sports Complex Andaman Water Sports Complex and Carbynscove Tourism Complex are the famous water sports complexes. The Gandhi Park Water Sports Complex and Andaman Water Sports Complex are organised and managed by the Department of Tourism, A&N Administration. All these water sports facilities are available on all week days. Two seater paddle boats, four seater paddle boats, kayaks, rowing boats, motor boats, sail yachts etc. are the types of boats given to tourists at very nominal rates for half-an-hour cruise duration. Snorkels, life jackets, lifebuoy etc. are also available in the complexes.

Adventure Sports Activities

Andaman waters are suitable for adventure water sports like scuba diving, skiing, sailing, Para-sailing, wind surfing, snorkeling, high sea game fishing etc. Trekking through the dense evergreen forests and Island camping in beach front forests are the other adventure activities.

Scuba Diving

Andaman waters offer a fascinating world of under-water marine life, varieties of colourful fishes, rarest of the coral reefs in the world, mysterious remains of sunken ships, etc. All these can be explored through Scuba Diving. Details regarding the authorised scuba diving centres, the areas opened for scuba diving and the terms and conditions for operating scuba diving centres can be obtained from the Directorate of Tourism.

Snorkeling

One can enjoy the under-water marine life and view the rarest varieties of corals by snorkeling near the Andaman Water Sports Complex, Corbyn's Cove Tourism Complex, Chidiyatappu, North Bay Islands in Mahatma Gandhi Marine National Park—(Jolly Buoy, Redskin), Cinque island, Havelock and Ross and Smith Islands

Swimming Pool

Till 1994, A&N Islands, the city has only one salt water swimming pool which was constructed inside the sea. One can swim in the pool when there is favourable tide. The Lt. Governor of A&N Islands has initiated and constructed another swimming pool inside the Gymkhana ground. It is beautiful looking, is of international standard and is really a wonderful facility provided to tourists. It is situated just a km. from bus terminus. Beside these swimming pools, the Hotel Bay Island of Welcome Group also has the swimming pool facility.

Other Facilities

There are 11 banks—10 commercial banks and one Cooperative Bank, with all facilities in A&N Islands. They have their branches in different Islands. The State Bank of India, Canara Bank, Syndicate Bank, Indian Overseas Bank, United Bank, UCO Bank, Punjab National Bank, Vijaya Bank, Andaman State Cooperative Bank, Indian Bank and Allahabad Bank are the major banks. The facility of exchanging foreign currency is limited to the main branch of State Bank of India and Indian Overseas Bank.

Next to Bank facilities, the A&N Administration through the Department of Health, headed by the Director of Health Services, provides hospitals/medical facilities. G.B.Pant Hospital is the biggest hospital with all its facilities situated in Port Blair just behind the Cellular Jail. Besides this hospital, there are amenities like Primary Health Centre, Community Health Centres, Sub-centres, Dispensary, Urban Health Centre, functioning in different places of these islands.

Shopping is another important activity of the tourists. They feel relaxed when they go for shopping. They want to buy and take the product which is the speciality of the particular destination. Port Blair city is famous for a variety of handicrafts. The tourists/visitors purchase handicrafts as mementoes for their friends and relatives with a pride that it is made in A&N Islands. Some tourists keep the product as a show piece in their own house as memory of visiting that place. Dancing dolls of different varieties, shell lamps, shell decoratives, shell hanging lamps, saree tops, table weights, shell saucers, pen stands, timber made fish, turtles, eagles, dinosaurs, shell made rings, necklace, kumkum pot etc. are very famous and specialised items of these Islands. Tourists spend a lot of amount on shopping.

Photography occupies an important place in tourism activity. Tourists do not get full satisfaction if they have not taken photos of the important places they liked and visited. Some tourists would like to have immediate developing and printing. Here in Andamans, photo studios, photographers, private video operators, video filming facilities are available. There are 58 Studios in Andaman and Nicobar Islands. Of them majority are situated in Port Blair city.

3

Historical Fascinations

Introduction

Tourists Fascinations, Classification of the fascinations, Types of Tourists, Economic and Non- Economic Tourists, Informational Fascinations, Dos and Don't Dos, Accommodations, both run by government and private sectors etc., have been presented in Chapter I and Chapter II. The Historical fascinations are given in the present chapter. After getting information about a particular place, everybody would like to know about the history of the place, its inception, and its population, importance and of all, the speciality of the place.

Historical Fascinations

The historical fascinations are the central characteristics and main attractions of the place. As far as Andaman and Nicobar Islands are concerned, the tourists are attracted mainly after learning basic information about the history of these islands. Sometimes tourists are briefed wrongly about the history of these islands in the Mainland. On some occasions, the author has also been asked the real history of these islands. The tourists coming to this place have expressed that they were briefed wrongly about this place, population — particularly the tribal population and the climate of these islands. Hence, it has been decided to give historical fascinations briefly in the present chapter. The historical fascinations are:

1. Location
2. History
3. Cellular Jail
4. Population and
5. Tribals

Location

Andaman and Nicobar Islands is one of the Union Territories of the Union of India. By virtue of its strategic geographical location in the Bay of Bengal and rich natural resources, it attracts and receives great attention. The Bay Islands, once coined as KALAPANI (the Black Waters) indicating the dreaded transportation and punishment of the British Government of India. The inhabitants of these islands are scattered far-flung and wide over a distance of 720 kms. Some of them are found established well in a few towns and innumerable small villages. The towns and small villages have started flourishing only recently, because of the harbour and airport facilities that have been established in these islands and will progress in shipping and other transport facilities. Andaman and Nicobar Islands today is a solid green paradise on the blue surface of Bay of Bengal, which stretches its long arm of welcome to the mainland as the tourism fascinations.

A&N Islands is situated in the Bay of Bengal and it is located between 6 degree and 14 degree of North latitude and 92 degree and 94 degree of East longitude. This, surrounded by Myanmar, Thailand, Malaysia, and Indonesia, constitutes the most isolated part of the Indian Union. These islands are parts of the continuous ridge that extends from Cape Nagrais in Burma (Myanmar) through Cocoa Islands and continues further south up to Sumatra. The southernmost tip of the territory is Indira Point (previously named as Pigmilion Point) in Great Nicobar which is only 146 kms. away from Sumatra. These islands comprise two separate groups, namely, the Andaman group of islands and the Nicobar group of islands with entirely different population and problems. The Andaman group of islands is separated from Nicobar group of islands by the boisterous 10 degree channel. The location of Andaman and Nicobar Islands is shown in maps II.1, II.2 and II.3. The seat of Administration of Andaman and Nicobar Islands is at Port Blair, the Capital of Andaman and Nicobar Islands which is connected with Kolkata by a sea distance of 1225 kms. and with Chennai by 1191 kms. and with Vishakhapatnam by 1200 kms.

A&N Islands comprising an area of 8293 sq.kms. are a group of picturesque islands. The land Area of Andaman group is 6340 sq.kms. 258 islands, large and small, constitute Andaman. Of these, North Andaman, Interview Islands, Middle Andaman, South Andaman, Little Andaman, Rut land etc. are large islands and hundred islands are yet to be named. The total land area of Nicobar group of islands is 1953 sq.kms. 61 Islands, large and small, make up the Nicobars, of which Car Nicobar, Teresa, Kamorta, Nancowry, Katchal, Little Andaman and Great Nicobar are large islands and 33 remain unnamed. It is to be mentioned here that in this group, the Great Nicobar has the largest area of about 1405 sq. kms. Of the total islands of this territory, only about 38 are inhabited.

History

The history of A&N Islands can be found in the decennial Census Reports, Louis 1912, Bonnington 1932 and other published works like those Klauss 1903 and Whitehead 1924. These give out a lot of information about this golden territory, Andaman and Nicobar Islands. People used to say many stories by combining fictions, imaginations, lies etc. to the other people who have never heard about these islands. It was told to the author before he visited these islands that "the mosquitoes are of the size of lemon. They hit the human population and malaria was the product of these islands. The coconuts are like big ball gourds. The coconuts will have atleast three litres of water. And more than 10 people are required to drink the water of one coconut and what not."

HISTORICAL FASCINATIONS

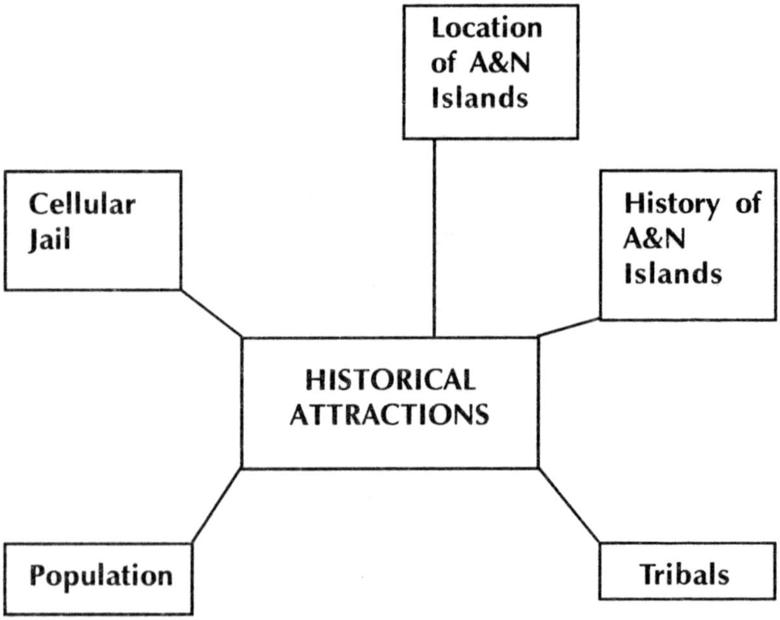

Some say that Tamilians were the first people who visited these islands, while some others say that it was the Malayalis that first came to these islands. The Malayalis sailed to Andamans with a view to capture the aborigines for their business activities. There are histories that the aborigines of these islands were captured and treated as slaves and were sold and purchased as trade goods. The first reliable historic reference to these islands is found in the writings of Chinese Buddhist Monk, I' Tsing made in 627 AD, who described these islands as "The land of the naked people". Later, mention of these islands is found in the collections of early Arab notes of the 9th century of India and China where the people of Andamans have been called "Angamainans"[1] and the people of Nicobar have been called "Lankabalus". The ancient Arab mariners mentioned that they bartered ambergris and coconut for iron[2]. In the earliest Hindu mythology the "Ramayana", the Andaman Islands were believed to be a land of "Hanuman". The Malayans used to refer to them as "Hanuman" and from Malaya, the knowledge of Andaman first spread to the different parts of the world. Claudius Pkole Macus (Ptolemy), a Roman Geographer located these islands on the map in the second century for the first time.

Probably the name, ANDAMAN, of the islands is a distorted form of HANUMAN, or "Monkey people", the aboriginal antagonists of the Aryan immigrants in India. Marco Polo, who passed by these islands in 1290, on his way to China, called these islands as "Angamanian". He observed that 'the local inhabitants "are the cruellest generation and eat anybody they can catch if not of their own race". Friar Ordoric, another European traveller who visited the Andamans in 1322, refers to the inhabitants of these Islands as "dog faced" and "cannibals". Nicolo Conti who came to Andamans in 1440, called these islands as "Andamania", the Islands of Gold.

East India Company had consolidated its hold in southern India by the middle of 18th century and the British were interested in having a place for shelter of ships in distress during the monsoon season. In 1777, John Ritchie reported that 'In whatever light these islands are considered, a thorough knowledge of them will appear to be a great utility. On 19th December 1788, Lt. Archibald Blair of the Indian Navy was deputed to survey the Andamans. After his day's survey, Lt. Archibald Blair reported that the port in South Andaman was suitable for settlement. On 12th June 1789, it was decided by the Governor General in Council to colonize these Islands. Blair sailed for the Andamans in September 1789 accompanied by some artificers, labourers and soldiers. By 25th October 1789, Blair was able to clear some land and put up the first settlement. In August, 1790, the settlers had almost cleared the site selected by Blair in Chatham Island where they planted vegetable and fruit trees. In November 1792, it was decided to move to a new settlement in North Andaman and the same was closed in May 1796. Again, on 11th November 1844, two ships were wrecked and 620 persons found themselves on an inhospitable island where they were constantly threatened by the tribal population. The

Andaman Committee was appointed to look into this matter with Dr. Frederick John Mount as the President. They examined various sites and then selected the place where the first settlement was set up by Blair. Actually, Blair was complimented for his sense of judgment and in honour of the first surveyor, this place was named as Port Blair. On 15th January 1845, it was decided by the Governor General in Council to establish a penal settlement on the Andamans for the reception in the first instance of Freedom Fighters sentenced to imprisonment and to transportation for the crime of Mutiny and rebellion and other offences connected therewith.

About the early history of the Nicobar group of islands, very little is known. The Chola kings of South India who had maritime interests came in contact with these islands. In the Great Thanjavur Inscription of 1050 AD, of Chola kings, the Nicobar Islands were referred to as "NAKAVARAM" which means the Land of the Naked. This was probably due to the appearance of these islanders, the body bare and a loin cloth with tail, hanging out. As far as the name of these islands is concerned, another history was also heard. That is when the Chola king visited these islands, he came with his group of people. When they were nearing an island a "MAAN" (deer) was standing there in the islands. They were able to see from far away. By standing in the boat/vessel they told in Tamil as "NICCUTHU PAR" that means "it stands see", when they saw the deer was standing. That Tamil phrase "NICCUTHU PAR" has become a "Nicobar". Again they went to the islands; they saw the people were searching for the deer, as they were the devotees of the "Lord Shiva" – the Greatest God, the most powerful God of the world. They could not find the deer which was standing on the island when these people were on the vessel. Normally, the devotees of Lord Shiva worship the divine animal deer. At present the deer is worshipped. Then after visiting the "NICCUTHU PAR" (Nicobar) Island, they started their journey from there. They were nearing the other island. Here also they saw a deer standing in the new island. They did not know actually, what was the name of the islands. But the group of people recollected the deers, which was standing in the "NICCUTHU PAR" (Nicobar) Island and conversed themselves and told in their language (Tamil) as MAAN, ANTHA MAAN. This means the same deer they have seen in the Niccuthu Par Islands, that deer is standing here also, that is, ANTHA MAAN. The Tamil term "ANTHAMAAN" might have become ANDAMAN. But there are no stories and histories about the Chola king's visit to Andaman and Nicobar Islands. From 16th century onwards, there have been frequent references to these islands in the writings of voyagers.

Traders from India, Burma, Penang and the Straits settlement came to these islands chiefly for coconuts. A&N Islands, especially Car Nicobar and Nancowry, gradually flourished as important trading centers. In 1711, the first attempt was made by French Jesuits, but they were not able to withstand and soon succumbed. In 1756, the Danes took possession of these islands for colonisation and set up their headquarters in Kamorta and till 1848 repeated attempts were made by them which finally failed. In 1869, the Nicobar Islands were taken over by the British with the consent of Denmark and a branch of Andaman penal settlement of 1869 was closed down in 1888 and the British were not interested in setting up an elaborate administrative structure in the Nicobar Islands due to continued expenditure, difficulties in maintaining the establishment and other reasons such as malarial climate, absence of moral, social and religious restraints and loss in transportation.

With the increased tempo of freedom movement, the number of prisoners, sent to the Andamans, went on increasing. With the Montford reforms of 1919, a general amnesty was granted to all the prisoners in the Andamans. But the rebellious outbursts in Burma and in the southern states of India kept the number of prisoners coming into Andamans on the increase. The constitutional reforms of 1935 necessitated a thorough revision of the policy. In September 1937, the first batch of prisoners left the Andamans and by January 1938, all the prisoners were released.

During the Second World War, the islands were under the Japanese occupation from March 1942 to October 1945. These islands were re-occupied by the British after the War. When India gained independence in 1947, A&N Islands remained annexed with her. The A&N Islands (Protection of Aboriginal Tribals) Act was passed in 1956, under which entry into tribal areas was prohibited and no outsider could carry on trade or industry in the islands without a license from the A&N Administration. Since November 1956, A&N Islands have been constituted into a Union Territory of India. Though geographically these islands are far apart from the mainland (of India), they constitute a part of the Indian Union and are administered by the President of India through Chief Commissioner upto 1983 and from 1984 onwards through Lt. Governor, whose headquarter is at Port Blair.

Population

The message about the population of these islands, particularly in present days, has a lot of historical importance and it attracts the people of the mainland. Since 2000 onwards, there has been a vast change in the characteristics of the group of the population. Till 1999, the Jarawas and Sentinalese were considered the most hostile tribals. With the help of the security forces, the officers and the ASI, Port Blair met the Jarawas with a view to give some eatables like coconuts and bananas. But from the year 2000 (year not known exactly) onwards, the Jarawas have been very friendly with the civilians. So, the population characteristics have been changing and the Sentinalese is the only hostile tribal. So, now the population consists of tribals, local population and settlers and government employees from mainland. The population of these islands is a heterogeneous one, with a mixture of diverse communities from the mainland. Today A&N Islands is a miniature India. People of all the states in India live in these Islands in harmony with their own culture. The actual population as per the year 2001, is 3,56,265 consisting of 3,14,239 in Andaman District and 42,026 in the Nicobar District. The total population includes male population to the extent of 1,92,985 and female population of 1,63,280.

POPULATION OF THE GREEN PARADISE (A&N ISLANDS)

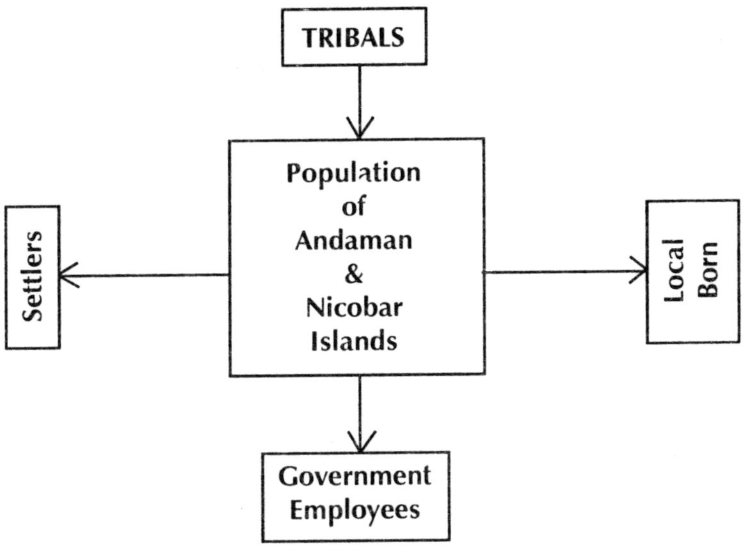

Groups of Population

As already mentioned, in A&N Islands people from different regions, religions, races, faiths etc. continue to live together in a peaceful manner. Some were invited to these islands and some came to these islands on employment and some started some economic activities of trade, commerce and industry. So the population of these islands can be broadly divided into following groups. They are:

Tribals,

Locals,

Settlers, and

Government Employees from the mainland.

These are discussed below:

Tribal Population

The tribals are classified into two major groups, namely Friendly Tribals and Hostile Tribals as far as free movement is concerned. On the basis of residential states, they are divided into two types, namely Andaman Tribals and Nicobar Tribals. Andaman Tribals are further divided into two types, as described earlier, namely friendly tribals and hostile tribals. They are given below:

Tribals

(i) Andaman Tribals

(ii) Nicobar Tribals.

I. Andaman Tribals

a. Friendly Tribals

b. Hostile Tribals

II. Nicobar Tribals

a. Friendly Tribals

b. Hostile Tribals.

I.a. Andaman Friendly Tribals

(i) Great Andamanese

(ii) Onges

(iii) Jarawas

I.b. Andaman Hostile Tribals

(i) Sentinalese

II.a. Nicobar Friendly Tribals

(i) Nicobarese

(ii) Shompens

II.b. Nicobar Hostile Tribals

There is no hostile type of tribals in the Nicobar Districts.

The aboriginals or the tribals of these islands are the original inhabitants of these far-flung islands. The total number of the tribal population as per 1991 census was 26,770 which is 9.5% of the total population of A&N Islands. The tribal population in numbers was not available for 1991 and not available for 2001 also. However, the growth rate of tribal population is given below:

Table : 3.1
Growth Rate of Tribal Population of A&N Islands

Year	Population	Growth Rate	% to the total Population
1951	12,145	-	39.2
1961	14,672	20.8	23.1
1971	18,102	23.4	15.7
1981	22,361	23.5	11.9
1991	26,770	19.7	9.5
2001	NA	NA	NA

Source : Compiled from the information collected.

As far as the number of individual tribals for the census years 1991 and 2001 are concerned, the census department of A&N Islands was contacted. They informed that they have not published the figures till date. They submitted a number of reasons for the delay in publication. However they have given the total number of tribal population of A&N Islands for the census year 1991 on the basis of which the author roughly calculated (though it is not correct) the growth rate and presented. The tribal population of these islands is divided into two, namely Andaman Tribals and Nicobar Tribals. A brief description of these tribals is given below:

Andaman Tribals

The aboriginals or the tribals of the Andaman Islands are known as Andaman Tribals. They are of Negrito stock/race.

Their main occupation is food gathering. Andaman and Nicobar Islands Tribals are of four types, namely:

1. Jarawas
2. Sentinalese
3. Onges, and
4. Great Andamanese.

JARAWAS

Among the four tribals, Jarawas are forest dwellers and were hostile. They inhabit and live in the west coast of South and Middle Andamans in the reserved forest area. They are said to be one of the purest and most primitive races in the world with human memory "who live on hunting and food gathering". The Jarawas did not have any relation with the other types of tribals and non-tribals and that's why nothing was known about their style of life and economy, habits and characteristics.

But now the situation has changed and has been changing. The Jarawas are no more dangerous. They have started to come closer to the non-tribals and the tribals of other races. They stand on the road. When the vehicles with passengers come/go, they also request the drivers to stop for a while. When the drivers stop their vehicles, all young Jarawas enter in and request the passengers for some eatables and chewable items particularly tobacco-based eatables. One more interesting thing is that they touch the bodies of the passengers and verify it with their body parts. Sometimes, they go to the extent of kissing the passengers also. When the passengers offer the eatables and chewable items, they express their happiness through laughing and soft touch etc. Another interesting thing is that they try to pick up the Hindi language. They do not do harm to anybody. They are not even rough in moving with the passengers. All these changes are noted when they are on the road. But one cannot simply take up these changes as the socio-economic and economic changes of the Jarawas. What will they do? How will they react? What will be the implementation of their real characterization? This can be known only when and find through a sustained contact and collating the impacts of association with these tribals.

TRIBAL POPULATION

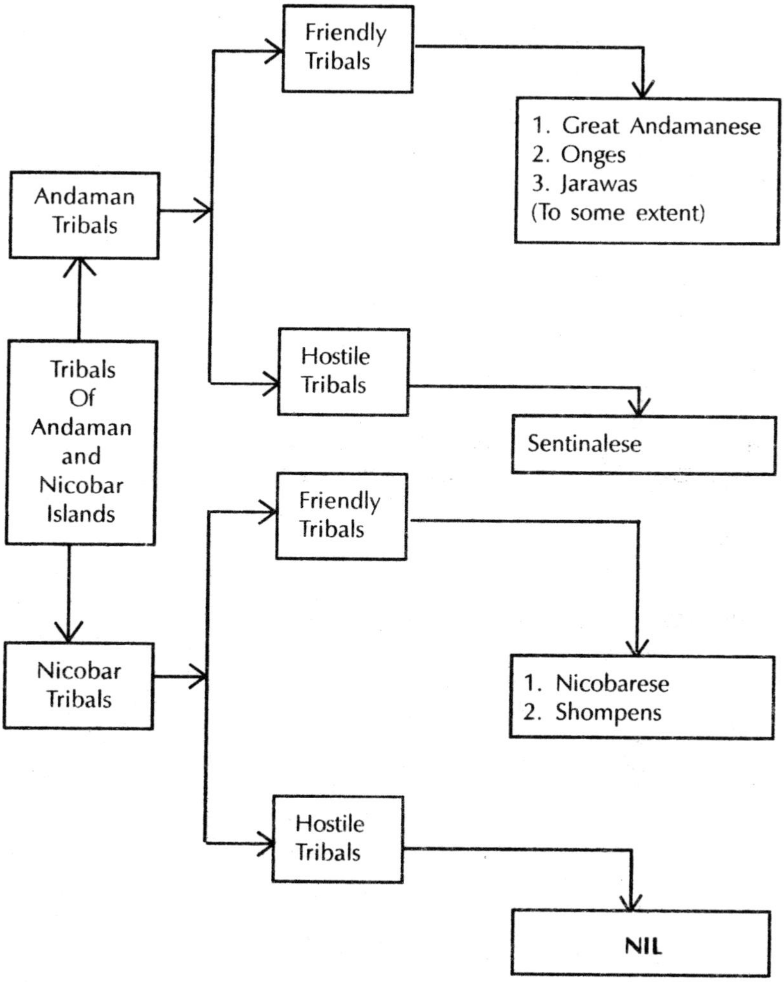

In apperance these tribals look dark like other Negrito tribes and have thick skin and long but curly hair. Both males and females are tall. It is understood that they love deer and like red colour. They do not wear dresses of any type. But they wear necklace, big mala, waist bands, head bands made out of sea-shells, palm leaves and some bones. Sometimes they decorate their bodies with clay. They collect fruit honey, tuber from different plants, fish monitor lizard, wild pig etc. for their food. But there is no evidence that they have killed deer and birds that are very friendly with Jarawas. Till 1973, the Jarawas could not be contacted. In 1974, the A&N Administration, through the joint efforts of anthropologists, successfully contacted one group of Jarawas and presented them gifts. From 1974 onwards, at intervals, the A&N Administration have been contacting the Jarawas and presenting them gifts, in the form of coconuts, red coloured clothes, drinking water, other eatables etc. No attempt, however, has been made to stay with them because the behaviour of the Jarawas is still unpredictable. Though there is a marked development in the characterization of the Jarawas as far as the free and friendly movement are concerned, one cannot take it for granted that they have become fully friendly with the non-Jarawas and non-tribals. They are to be studied more thoroughly and over a period of contacts and stay overs.

Sentinalese

The Sentinalese are also forest dwellers who are very hostile. They are unapproachable. They inhabit and live in the isolated island named North Sentinel Island, situated in the west direction to the Port Blair City. The Sentinalese are left alone in the reserved small island, the area of which is about 50 sq. kms. It is very interesting to note that their huts have fire-burning sticks with the safety fencing. Their inner fencing may be to prevent any accident during sleeping hours. The approximate measurement of the huts is as follows –

Height (Front) – 2.25m   Length – 2.25m

Height (Back) – 1.25m   Breadth – 1.50m

The Sentinalese live in small sized huts under trees. They use arrow and bow, plucking stick, arrow-cum-spear, bamboo pot, nautilus shells, fishing net, cane basket, waist band, grinding stone, hammer stone, resin, pig skull, dug out canoe, multi-pronged wooden harpoon spear etc. to serve their various purposes.

Onges

Among the Andaman tribes, Onges are the friendliest type. They inhabit and live in the Little Andaman Islands and came in contact with the outside civilization, following the setting up of the settlement. They are very friendly with the non-tribals. Occasionally, they come out of their residence or islands. Now a days, they speak good Hindi and move with the non-tribals in a free and friendly way. "They are of dark colour, short statured with unusual growth of buttocks (both males and females). Their hands and feet are small but strong. Their eyes are bright and clear white in contrast to their complexion. Their teeth are remarkably strong and are retained till old age though not regularly cleaned". Most of the Onges are very weak and some of them suffer from a disease like tuberculosis. Now the A&N Administration has opened a dispensary and individual health cards are being maintained. The local administration has constructed some modern double storeyed residential houses for them. They call themselves "Onges", a verbal noun meaning of "Man Being". The interesting point is that they now have started demanding the administration to do something for their better socio-economic and cultural development. Some of them demand jobs also.

But they are in a minority. Their actual number is not known. Another important point to be noted is that they had no proper concept of dressing. Compared with the males, the females used the indigenous "nakuinyage", a tassel made of tender palm leaves to cover their genitals. But now, they wear beautiful and coloured dresses. Another unique feature of Onges is to go for shiny painting their bodies. Both the sexes paint themselves, but it is the work of the female to paint her husband. Red colour paint is used at the time of bad events like death and rituals etc. but painting with white clay is used at the time of happiness like love, festivals, celebrations, hunting etc. A female Onge has to paint her husband's body and face immediately after the marriage with white clay. It is believed that more time consumed to paint means that the wife loves the husband more. These days, too, the same traditions are followed but one can see the decline too. They have begun to wear modern dresses. As far as their economic activities are concerned, pig hunting, collection of forest produce, fishing, construction of huts, and preparation of dug out canoes and catching turtles are the primary ones. They also do their own cooking and eating.

Great Andamanese

Other Andaman friendly tribes are the Great Andamanese. Great Andamanese are also one of the Negrito race. They are beautiful and handsome to look at. They are very friendly with the non-tribals and tribals of other races. There are ten groups, namely Cari, Kora, Jero, Bo, Kedo, Kol, Juwai, Bojiayab, Bea, and Balawa.

Great Andamanese wear all types of dresses including T-shirts available in the market. The number of Great Andamanese has started declining. They speak good Hindi and understand English too. They have even started finding fault with the government for not providing them facilities. On 6th December 2002, the ASI celebrated their Golden Jubilee Year and organised a seminar on social changes in Andaman and Nicobar Islands. Two Great Andamanese women participated and expressed their problems, even demanding more job opportunities for them.

At one time, they dominated the full South Andaman Islands with an estimated population of 5000 but due to the ill-treatment meted out by the authorities, their strength has come down to 26 as per the 1981 census. The main reason for this is the contact of non-tribals. "Great Andamanese were enjoying a free, independent and healthy life, free from disease. But the contact with the outside world brought epidemics like cholera, small pox, measles and other contagious diseases like T.B. V.D. etc." Great Andamanese are short in height. The men's average height is 5'1" (approx.) and that of their women is 4'7" (approx). The chests of the men are muscular. The colour of their skin is light black.

Nicobar Tribals

The aboriginal or the tribals of the Nicobar Islands are known as Nicobar Tribals. They are completely different from Andaman

Tribals. All are friendly with non-tribals and tribals of other race. Their main occupation is also food gathering. Nicobar Tribals are of two types, namely Nicobarese and Shompens.

Nicobarese

Among the tribal population of A&N Islands, the Nicobarese are the advanced and most civilized and developing tribe. They wear good dresses and use cosmetics to be at par with non-tribals. They love one another and non-tribals as well. Now-a-days, they get employment in almost all the government jobs. They are free and frank in their approach. Even they have started marrying non-tribals particularly mainlanders. They inhabit and live in almost all the parts of Nicobar group of islands. They live in fairly well-organised communities. Most of the Nicobarese are living in Car Nicobar and to a less extent in Nancowry and Katchal.

Shompens

Another type of primitive tribes of Nicobar tribals is the Shompens. They inhabit the Great Nicobar Island. They are not like Jarawas, Sentinalese, Onges or Great Andamanese who belong to Negrito race. But Shompens are from Mongoloid race. They live in interior jungles and are very shy to come in front of any human not belonging to their race. They eat coconuts, bananas, pandanus, tubers, fish, wild pig, lizards etc. The Shompens do have business relations with the Nicobarese. The local administration has provided infrastructural facilities and helps the Shompens to lead a peaceful life. A&N Administration has opened a school in their area to give formal and informal education.

Andaman Indians (The Local Born)

The Andaman Indians are the people of the mainland who have settled in the islands mainly in South Andaman under unusual circumstances. When A&N Islands were under penal settlement, i.e. during 1858-1945, the entire population of A&N Islands except the tribals or aboriginal consisted of Freedom

Fighters, administrative personnel concerned with the Freedom Fighters, merchants, etc. The Freedom Fighters formed the major portion of the population. The penal settlement was abolished in the year 1945 by remitting all sentences and offering repatriation. The local born were recorded as Andaman Indians in the 1951 census. A&N Gazetteer of 1908 describes the local born as descendants of Freedom Fighters born in the settlement and permanent residents there. Bonnington (1931:19) described local population or community as descendants from Indian Freedom Fighters parents on both sides who had settled in Andamans. They have been characterized by strong unity among themselves and also constitute an amalgamated society. They have separate reservations in seat allotment for pursuing higher education to go to mainland as well as in getting jobs in these islands.

New Settlers

The New Settlers include colonisers who are mainly refugees from East Bengal, Bihar and Kerala. They settled permanently on cleared forest land which is suitable for agriculture and pastoral occupations. At present the settlers do business in various forms like cultivation, producing vegetables, work in factories, business, mines and quarries etc. Some settlers have constructed good houses and rented them out. By and large, the settlers lead a very happy life in these islands.

Government Employees

This is the most dominating group. This group of population includes persons who have come to these islands from the mainland on government employment, transfer, deputation etc. This group includes employees of A&N Administration ranging from secretaries to clerks, teachers and employees of Schools, colleges, institutes and institutions, all doctors and related personnel of hospitals and dispensaries, employees of banks, Public Works Department, all departments of A&N Administration, Govt. of India, Defence, Telecommunications, Census, Anthropological Survey of India, Botanical Survey of India, Zoological Survey of India etc.

Port Blair City

Port Blair City is the gateway to Andaman and Nicobar Islands. This is the only city in the A&N Islands. It is the constituent like cities of India. Port Blair is the nerve centre of the economy of A&N Islands and hence the development of this city will indirectly influence the growth and economic development of other islands and centres. Port Blair city is located in the south-east portion of South Andaman division. Port Blair city derives its name from Archibald Blair, a brilliant surveyor who was commissioned by the British govt. in the 18th century for a penal settlement.

Since it is the capital of the state of A&N Islands, its administrative headquarters is situated in the city. It is the most important business and market centre of this territory and is the seat of most of the govt. offices of these islands, Central Govt. and public and private bodies. Port Blair City is an important harbour in the islands, handling most of their cargo and the passenger traffic. The Chatham harbour and Haddo are the two important harbours. The city has an airport too. Earlier, Indian Airlines was the only carrier to fly here. However, from 22.11.1996, Alliance Ltd., a subsidiary company of Indian Airlines Corporation and Jet Airways Ltd. also operate its air service between Chennai – Port Blair – Chennai sectors. In 2001, the Government of India constructed and opened a marvellous airport of International Standard. The name given to the airport is Veer Savarkar Airport. The airport contains all facilities. The total geographical area of the town is about 7.9 sq.kms. It has 57 revenue villages with a population of 74,955 as per 1991 census. About 26.7 per cent of total population of A&N Islands is living in this city.

The population of Port Blair City is 1,09,617 as per the 2001 census. It consists of 60,528 males and 49,089 female including child population (0-6 years) of 12,430. The literates are 84,347.The occupational aspect of the city is divided into five categories, namely govt. employees, teachers in schools and colleges, owners of small-scale industrial units, trades, skilled workers, labourers etc. Taxis and govt. transport buses are the only mode of travel and means of written communication. The Port Blair city has a lot of tourist fascinations and places of historic interest and significance, its scenic beauty attracts a large number of tourists both from mainland and abroad. The important places and places of tourist interest in Port Blair city are marked in the city map.

Cellular Jail

This is the main historical place of this green paradise. The cellular jail is the actual molecule behind the historical importance of these golden green islands. But the cellular jail itself has a long history to tell all our "Nation Lovers". Each particle of sand will have a lot to tell. The patriots who raised their voice against the British were sent to this Jail where many perished. In this Cellular Jail, freedom fighters like Veer Savarkar, Baba Prithvi Singh Azad, Bhai Parmanand, Ullash Kar Datta, T. Sacchidanada Sivam, and host of others faced inhuman torture and humiliation at the hands of David Barrie and other Jailors.

The Cellular Jail is a national memorial. It is located in Port Blair– 2 kms. from Port Blair bus terminus. It is the most important landmark of Port Blair and even India. This is known as Bastille of India and relic of bygone years where India's freedom fighters were incarcerated. The Cellular Jail brings back to the mind of the tourists a saga of struggle for emancipation of people kept in bondage by the alien power, how the Indian Freedom Fighters were punished through the flogging stand, how they were killed by the British jailors and how our freedom fighters were humiliated to work. The tourists can see the photographs attached. The construction of the Cellular Jail had originally begun in 1896 but was completed in 1906. It took 10 years to complete the construction. The cellular jail was constructed with three storeyed long wings in seven numbers, starting from the Central Tower from where one can see the seven wings. The size of each cell was and is 7 x 13.5 feet (that is 7 feet breadth and 13.5 length). Each cell has a ventilator sized 3 x 1 feet at a height of 10 feet. The spirit of our Indian freedom fighters still lives on here though they were vigorously murdered and killed by the merciless jailors appointed by the British government. If anyone comes and witnesses the light and sound programme in Hindi language organised in the Cellular Jail, he/she will be aggressively irritated against the unprincipled management of those jailers and their animal characteristics.

The Jail acquired the name 'Cellular' because it is entirely made up of individual cells for the solitary confinement of the prisoners. The cells tell the stories of the sufferings, sacrifices and indomitable courage on the part of freedom fighters incarcerated in it. The detailed lists of freedom fighters of the first war of independence, who were transported to the penal settlement of Andaman Islands (only available names) state-wise, Wahabi Rebels, Freedom fighters incarcerated in Cellular Jail from (1909-1921). Freedom fighters incarcerated in Cellular Jail from (1922-1932) 1932-1938, Moplah rebels deported to Andaman (1922-1924), martyrs during (1942-1945), are given below for reference to tourists. The Cellular Jail had 698 cells. Due to an earthquake, the Cellular Jail suffered damage in four wings and at present only three out of seven prongs are intact. The damaged portions had been earmarked for the construction of hospital and now the G.B. Pant hospital is functioning there.

Now the Cellular Jail has been declared as a national monument since 11th Feb, 1979. The saga of this heroic struggle is now brought alive in a Moving son at Lumiere (sound and light show). The Department of Tourism runs such show based on the history of this island and jail as if it is told by the oldest "peepal tree", still inside the Jail. The Cellular Jail has now become the place of pilgrimage for all the freedom loving people etc. Timings to go around the Cellular Jail during all days is between 9 A.M. and 5 P.M. with a lunch break between 12 noon and 1 P.M. The photographs of the Cellular Jail are given for the purpose of the tourists.

Light and Sound Programme (organised in the Cellular Jail)

After reaching the destination, tourists are always curious to know how things are produced, made, what the history was etc. The history of our freedom struggle can never be completed without telling the real story of today's Cellular Jail and yesterday's building of sufferings. Actually the name of the jail is Cellular but should have been called Sold (Sell) our Soul Jail. Truly speaking our freedom fighters sold (sacrifice) their soul to earn our freedom. Freedom fighters in the Jail were troubled, tortured, tormented, and grieved physically and mentally by the merciless British jailors. Our Indian freedom fighters were given garbage water to drink, were punished for many things failing which they were iron boxed, beaten by locking in flogging stand and what not. If somebody narrates about a memorial, to what extent a tourist understands depends upon the mediating language, the way in which he puts it, time and situation in which they interact etc. But when a tourist watches the Light and Sound Programme, which is being conducted in the Cellular Jail, a national memorial, he becomes knowledgeable. The programme is in both the languages, Hindi and English, and is shown every day in the evening.

4

Socio - Cultural Fascinations

Introduction

Tourists fascinations, Informational fascinations and Historical fascinations have been presented in the previous chapters. Next to these fascinations, the socio-cultural fascinations are very important to attract people magnetically from different places of the world in the name of tourists. Social and cultural fascinations are the powerful machines to convert the ordinary public into an economic tourist. The mixed culture of the population of these islands and their style of social life are the example of the national integration. Here, the specialty is that the people of all religions and regions are living without any difference of opinion. The tourists are attracted heavily by the social fascinations and cultural fascinations. It is quite natural that people would like to know the new style of life and the new sophisticated culture, traditions, customs, ceremonies, music, religious belief, cuisine of a new place. So an attempt has been made to highlight the socio-cultural aspects of the people of these islands.

Social and Cultural Fascinations

Social and cultural development and tourism development are inter-related. Social and cultural development will attract more tourists and tourism is an important medium of social cultural development. Socio-cultural fascinations are real tourist fascinations not only for the pleasant point of view but also from educational point of view. The social and cultural activities are the real and original reflectors of the qualities of the people/ society. They are the working tangible assets of any country and so the case of the A&N Islands also. The socio–cultural activities are the most important motivating and influencing factors on the tourists to visit these islands. The mixed culture and social life of the people of A&N Islands attract the majority of the tourists who have a desire to see something new and visualise something different from their own experience.

The A&N Islands is a new world, owned by India, having different patterns of life, manners, habits, social traditions, cultural traditions, hospitality, peace, festivals etc., with attractive sites and scenes. Next to the social and cultural activities, fairs and festivals of a particular place play an important role. Fairs and festivals are always associated with joy and happiness and are the best way of entertaining the people of all age groups since these are occasions on which they gather, assemble, exchange their views, work together, worship their Gods, etc. This has been an important part of the human life since olden days. The Social and Cultural fascinations are discussed under the following headings:

1. Peaceful Religions
2. Integrated Life style
3. Fairs and Festivals

Peaceful Religions

The religious personality of A&N Islands is very complex since it is a miniature India. People of different regions from different states have been living in this territory with the aborigins of this place. Hindus, Muslims, Christians, Sikhs, Buddhists, Jains, Bhahais etc. are the major religions of these islands. There are 22 temples, 9 churches, 4 masjids etc. in and around Port Blair. It is found that the tourists of every religion go to their religious centres i.e., temple, church, mosque, gurudwara etc., as and when they reach Port Blair.

Another point to be mentioned here is that some people, with inborn qualities go to all religious centres and worship all gods irrespective of their religion. Now a days, the practice has started growing not only in Port Blair but also in majority of the places of these islands. The way of organising and celebrating poojas and the method of worshipping their respective gods by the people of these islands are the special fascinations drawing the minds of the tourists from nooks and corners of the mainland. The numbers of religious centres in and around Port Blair are given in the following table:

Table : 4.1
The number of religious centres in and around Port Blair

S. No.	Particulars/Classification of the Centres	Number
01	Temples	22
02	Masjids	04
03	Churches	09
04	Gurudwaras	02
05	Baba Temple	01
06	Bhahai Temple	01
07	Buddhist Temple	01
	Total	**40**

Source : Dr. N. Rajavel's *Tourism in A&N Islands,* 1998

Integrated Life-style

An A&N Island is a place where people from all states of India are living together. They are from different religions and they live in perfect harmony and brotherhood. Tourists can study the social, cultural life of this territory. The society of these islands consists of three groups, namely, Friendly Tribals, Local Borns, Settlers and Govt. Employees, etc. (please see the Historical fascinations Chapter for details). All these groups mix freely with one another, even cutting across caste and religious boundaries. They love one another and try to find their own solution for their common problems and sometimes they help the local administration also by solving many complex issues related to the regions and religions etc.

The vigorous and importance of religions and regions among these three groups is slightly disappearing because marriages between people of North and South are becoming common. For example, a Hindu or Muslim from North will marry a Christian or Muslim of South and the like. Not only this type of marriages, also marrying tribals by the non-tribals and marrying the non-tribals by the tribals is also on the increase. All regional and religious functions are celebrated in almost all the families. Other private functions like celebration of Marriages, Birthdays, House warming, Anniversaries etc. one can find people from all religions and regions. They socialize frequently. Respect for other religions has almost become an accepted feature of the socio-culture of these islands.

Fairs and Festivals

Fairs and festivals have an important role to play in the A&N Islands and particularly in the field of tourism. Sometimes tourists stay back for a week in order to see the fairs and festivals. While they plan to travel to these islands, they extend their stay after seeing the impressive fairs. In this tourist paradise, fairs and festivals are celebrated in almost all parts. Generally, fairs are related to Govt. programmes as Islands on March, Trade Fairs, Navy Mela exhibition etc. As far as the festivals are concerned the A&N Administration celebrates one important festival, namely Andaman Tourism Festival.

People of concerned religious groups celebrate the remaining festivals. There is no doubt, that all religions celebrate their own festivals according to their economic condition and style, yet some festivals are more popular in A&N Islands. People from all religious groups participate in one another's festival without any hesitation. Here Hindus, Muslims, Christians and Sikhs are all equal. This unity is a speciality given by history and goes a long way in promoting the socio-cultural integrated festivals in A&N Islands. Besides the religious festivals like Deepavali, Ramzan, Christmas etc., among the popular festivals, the most important festivals are linked with Hindu culture, traditions and faith. They are:-

1. Ayappa Pooja
2. Christmas
3. Deepavali
4. Durga Pooja
5. Ganesh Pooja
6. Gokula Ashtami
7. Gurunanak Jayanti
8. Holi
9. Kali Pooja
10. Mariamman Thiruvizha
11. Nag Panchami
12. Panguni Utthiram
13. Pongal
14. Pradhosha Pooja
15. Ram Navami
16. Ramzan
17. Sankata Hara Chaturthi Pooja
18. Saraswati Pooja
19. Shivaratri
20. Vasanta Panchami
21. Villakku Pooja

Their importance is discussed here.

SOCIAL & CULTURAL FASCINATIONS

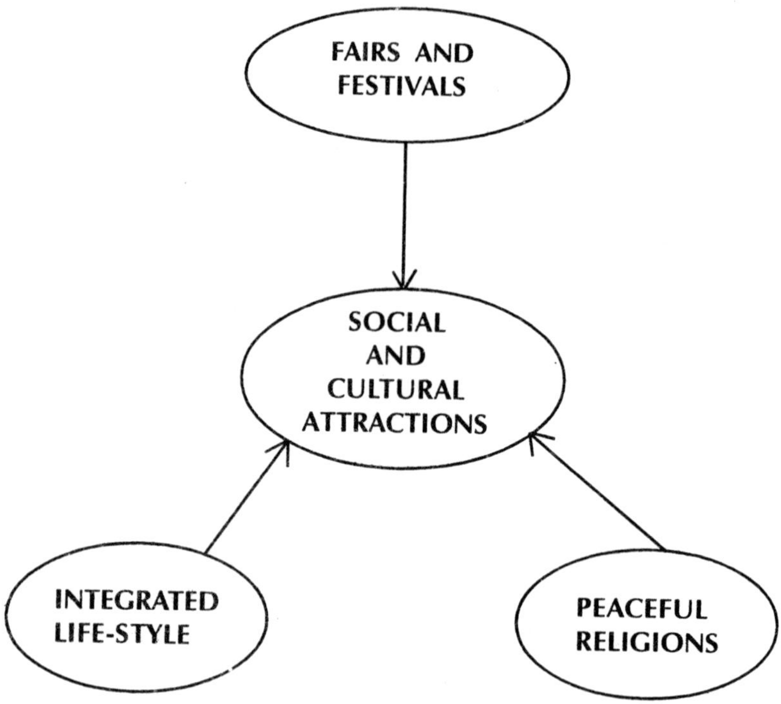

AYAPPA POOJA

Ayappa pooja is celebrated every year on 14th or 15th January depending upon the date of Thai 1st (Tamil month). The devotees observe for a period of 45 to 60 days preceding the 1st day of the Thai month. All Ayappa devotees perform poojas three times a day starting from 5 O'clock in the morning (for 45 days to 60 days). On Thai 1st, the devotees go to Ayappa temple to worship Lord Ayappa. During these days, bhajans, songs about Ayappa with the clappings and other musical instruments is performed during pooja time. It is very interesting to see the strong belief that this pooja and worship bring the blessings of Lord Ayappa.

DURGA POOJA

This is also an important festival of Hindus celebrated with great enthusiasm in the Hindu calendar month of Ashweis. This Pooja is celebrated by all Hindus in the name of Navaratri Pooja for nine days. Every year Durga Pooja is celebrated in these islands during the months of September-October. Bengali associations in each village and some organisations make the images of Goddess Durga in a highly decorative manner out of clay along with the images of other gods like Sri Ganesh, Sri Karthik (Sri Murugan) etc. and they perform pooja with the help of priests.

GANESH POOJA

All people other than aboriginal have been celebrating this pooja as a festival. Ganesh Pooja is celebrated in the Hindu calendar month of Bhadrapad Sudha Chaturthi every year. People from the south call this Pooja "Vinayaga Chaturthi". People buy Ganesh idols according to their requirements. The Ganesh temples at Aberdeen Bazaar, Goal Ghar etc. are beautifully decorated and the priests, Iyers or pujaris, perform special poojas or 'Arti' in Honour of God Ganesh. Of all the Ganesh temples, Sri Lakshmi Vinayagar Temple at Aberdeen Bazaar and Shri Karpaga Vinyagar at Goal Ghar are the chief fascinations on the occasion. Generally, the pooja is celebrated for three days. The temples are full of devotees (Bhakta). During the pooja, people offer "Kozhukattai' and "Sundal" to the deity "Vinayagar" and after the pooja, the Kozhukattai and Sundals are distributed among the devotees present. Some organisations and offices or groups of people also perform common pooja. A big image of God Ganesh is installed at an important place in the village or organisations erect special pandals for community poojas. Temples are brimming with devotees on all three days. People from other religions also visit the temple with their family members.

There is no distinction of caste, colour and creed to celebrate this pooja as a festival in these islands. A dish prepared out of rice flour, jaggery and coconut called ''Kozhukattai' is offered to Lord Ganesh as an important item of Pooja Prasad. Another dish prepared from boiled Chana (gram) and fried with mustard is called "Sundal".

GOKULA ASHTAMI

It is celebrated in the Hindu calendar month of Shravan Bahula Ashtami as the birthday of Lord Krishna who is regarded as the eighth incarnation of Lord Vishnu. This festival usually falls in the month of August-September. In Radha Krishna, Radha Govinda Temples on RGT Road, Sri Krishna Temple in Dairy Farm, Radhakrishna Temple in Junglighat, this festival is celebrated with great enthusiasm. Temples are fully illuminated with lights and coloured lamps. Group bhajans, songs on Krishna, continuous pooja performance with high clappings, with loud sayings like "Krishna Ki Jai" and other performances continue till midnight when Sri Krishna was born. After the birth, pooja is performed and prasad made of sweet sooji, sweet boondi, bananas, and sugarcane etc. are distributed. All temples are crowded with devotees and tourists.

SHRI GURUNANAK JAYANTI

The Punjabis celebrate this festival with great enthusiasm. It commemorates the birthday of Sikh Guru Sri Guru Nanak. This festival is celebrated according to the Hindu calendar on Karthik Poornima day. Police Gurudwara in Aberdeen Bazaar, Dr. Diwan Singh Gurudwara, just behind the State Bank of India, Main Branch, MES Gurudwara in MES area are illuminated beautifully. Songs, prayers, readings, bhajans etc. are the special features on the occasion. They organise a simple but excellent, calm procession with the songs and bhajans with the sayings "Gurunanakji ki jai". Both men and women participate in the procession on four-wheelers. The way they organise it is very attractive.

HOLI

According to the Hindu calendar, this festival falls on Phalguni Poornima day which usually falls during the month of February -March. In Holi is celebrated by the people of all age groups irrespective of the religion and region. When the people of A&N Islands play Holi one can see the enthusiasm and happiness on their faces during the festival of colours. Some people go to the temple while the youngsters go to watch movies.

SRI KALI POOJA

This festival is associated with the worship of Goddess Maa Kali as the Goddess of ruining the evils. In the Hindu calendar, this comes in the month of Aswin, which falls in the months of October-November. The Bengalis take keen interest and celebrate it enthusiastically. Kali temple at Prem Nagar is decorated beautifully with coloured lamps. Prescribed pooja and artis are performed. A lot of Hindus particularly Bengalis. visit this temple and other places where the images of Goddess Maa Kali are installed and worshipped. Next day, the image is taken in the form of a procession with songs and dances, to Haddo Jetty, Aberdeen Jetty and/or Junglighat Jetty for immersion. A large crowd assembles to witness the procession at Goal Ghar, opposite to State Library, Junglighat Junction, Dairy farm Junction, Aberdeen Bazaar, Delanipur, Haddo etc.

SRI MARRIAMMAN THIRUVIZHA (FESTIVAL)

This is the second biggest festival of Hindus celebrated in honour of Goddess Arulmigu Sri Mariamman. This temple is situated in Astinabad village, at a distance of six kms. from Port Blair bus terminus on Chidiyatappu route. The belief of all the people from all religions is that Goddess Mariamman has been guarding these islands. There is a famous lore here that when the Dhannikari Dam was being constructed, the contractor could not complete it successfully due to frequent cracks and scratches. Then he prayed to Goddess Mariamman by wearing Sedal ornaments and he saw Goddess Mariamman in his dream and she encouraged him to continue his efforts. After the completion of the dam, the contractor constructed the present temple (RCC building) and deposited some amount of money in the temple's name for daily conduct of pooja, celebrations and maintenance. Now, all people irrespective of their religion and region visit this temple and worship Goddess Mariamman. All tourists, including foreigners, do not leave these islands without offering prayers in these two temples. The festival is celebrated every year during the month of February. For Goddess Mariamman also, the devotees perform pooja and aarti in the same manner as offered to God Sri Vetrimalai Murugan. Theemithi, Arugandam Kavady, Parakkum Kavady, Pal Kavady, Panneer Kavady, Ilaneer Kavady are the special fascinations for the people, devotees and tourists. The terms "Parakkum" means flying, "Pal" means milk, "Theemithi" means walk on fire, "Arugandam" means troublesome, "Ilaneer" means tender coconut.

PANGUNI UTTIRAM

This festival has great importance among the people of these islands. This festival is celebrated to honour God Sri Vetrimalai Murugan (God Karthik), the son of Lord Shiva and Goddess Parvati. Sri Vetrimalai (victory hill) Murugan Temple is the oldest temple in these islands. The important feature of this temple is that, the people of all region and religions of our country and foreign tourists visit this temple. The strong belief of the people is that their requests are fulfilled and graced by God Murugan. During the festival, the temple is decorated with colourful lights and banners. During the festival period, every day 'Anna Dhanam' is performed. About 10,000 to 15,000 people come to the temple to take part in the Anna Dhanam (i.e. they eat full meal). Tourists can witness God Vetrimalai Murugan's divine powers. People from other islands flock to Port Blair to take part in this celebration. The roads from Haddo to Vetrimalai Murugan temple are full of people. People of all religions offer lime juice, orange juice, salted sweet water, butter milk, and water to all the devotees, visitors, tourists etc. as a partial fulfilment of their promises. The Sedal and Kavady bearers walk on fire (Theemithi) and reach the "Moolasthanam". One can't stand near the fire even at a distance of 6 mtrs. Devotees walk on the fire which means every body should accept the supreme power of the God Sri Vetrimalai Murugan. The term "Moolasthanam" means the place where the God's statue is situated.

PRADHOSHA POOJA

This is one of the very important poojas celebrated and offered to Lord Shiva. It is celebrated in all Shiva temples. This pooja was not given much importance till 1999. Since 2000 onwards, the islanders have realized the Importance of Pradhosha Pooja. There are two Pradhosha Poojas every month. One is celebrated during the period of waxing moon and the other during the period of depreciating moon. Lord Shiva will be decorated with his wife, Goddess Parvati next to him. The security position of Lord Shiva, that is, Nandi Dev (Bhagwan) will also be decorated. The devotees will present rice to Nandi Dev (Bhagwan) and the same (rice) will be distributed as Prasad to all the others present in the temple. Normally, devotees mix jaggery with rice and cardamom to offer as sweet. The speciality of the Pradhosha Pooja is that all demands of the devotees are sent through the security Bhagwan, Sri Nandi Dev which will be granted by Lord Shiva. So, the devotees, immediately after the Aarti, whisper their demands and requests to Nandi Dev (in its ear) to forward the same to Lord Shiva for the boons to be granted. On these days one can see long queues of devotees in the temple.

PRAKASH YATRA

This is celebrated just a day before Christmas by going in a long procession. Christians from all churches participate in the celebration. About 6000 Christians participate in the celebration/ procession. Both males and females participate and each participant carries a lighted candle by saying some slogans of the Holy Bible. The procession is on foot and is performed in a very calm and peaceful manner. Crowd gathers at different places to witness the procession.

RAM NAVAMI

In the Hindu calendar, Ram Navami is celebrated in the month of Chaitra, which falls in the month of March-April. It is celebrated as Lord Ram's birthday. Special poojas and Aartis are performed in Ram Temples located in Aberdeen Basthi, Kumrakheti, Haddo and Dairy Farm. This day is recognised as a festival day. Temples are decorated with colourful lights and musical instruments are played, songs on Lord Ram and Sita are also presented.

SANKATAHARA CHATURTHI POOJA

This pooja is offered to Lord Sri Ganesh. The meaning of the pooja – the term "sankat" means "difficulties, problems, sorrows, trials, straits, troubles, sufferings and narrowness" and the term "Hara" means "to put away or to remove". So, to remove their difficulties, the devotees offer poojas to Lord Sri Ganesh. This Pooja is performed on the fourth day from the full moon day. This pooja is performed at the time of the rising moon too. The devotees offer Kozhukattai, Pongal, Sundal, Laddu etc. to Lord Sri Ganesh which is later distributed after the Aarti as Prasad to all devotees present in the temple. There is a huge rush in the temple on these days. This pooja is organised and performed in all the Ganesh temples on these islands.

SARASWATI POOJA

It is a common festival celebrated with great gusto irrespective of religion. Saraswati pooja is another festival celebrated by all individuals, educational institutions, organisations like Post Office etc. in these islands, and is associated with the worship of Goddess Maa Saraswati, the Goddess of education and vidhdhai (vidhya) knowledge. Continuous Pooja and Arti are performed throughout the day. All students, public, tourists, employees worship the Goddess Maa Saraswati. A large crowd assembles to witness the procession of immersion.

SRI SHIVARATRI

This is another very important festival celebrated in these islands which falls in the Hindu calendar month of Magha, mainly February-March. Lord Shiva Temples in Delanipur, Pahar Goan, and Garacharma perform special Poojas and Aartis with usual decorations. In Sri Vetrimalai Murugan Temple the Shiva

Lingam is specially adorned with colourful flowers meant for Lord Shiva. In all Lord Shiva Temples, bhajans, kirtana, sweet songs, speeches, talks, dramas, video films on Shiva Parvati continue throughout the night.

SHASHTHI FESTIVAL

This festival falls on the sixth day after Diwali, in the Hindu calendar of Karthik. Devotees purchase Laksharchana Tickets costing from Rs. 101 – Rs.151. Tourists visit these islands during this festival period, purchase tickets, participate in pooja and take the Prasad to their native village/country as a divine symbol of Sri Vetrimalai Murugan, Port Blair, A&N Islands.

VILLAKKU POOJA

This is one of the oldest poojas organised only by the Hindus. So far this pooja has been organised by the families of the Hindu devotees at their houses. This is performed by married women. The person who organises the Villakku Pooja in her house will call many Sumangalis of different Hindu families to her house every Friday, preferably in the (growing moon) waxing moon period and perform pooja. "Sumangali" means a married woman living with her husband. This Villakku Pooja is offered to Goddess Maa Maha Lakshmi. This was the custom prevalent sometime back. Now a days, in these islands, Villakku Pooja has become a community celebration. All temples particularly Shri Ganesh Temple at Dairy farm, Shri Vetrimalai Murugan Temple, Port Blair and Mariyamma Temple at Astinabad, have started celebrating the Villakku Pooja. All Sumangalis go to these temples with their Kutthu Villakku and other articles like flowers, kumkum, oil, turmeric, sugar candy etc. The Sivachariyar (priests) will arrange the place for each participant and pooja will begin. All Sumangalis will have to recite the verses very carefully with the priest. This pooja will continue for more than two hours and at the end of it prasad is distributed to all devotees.

OTHER FESTIVALS

Other Hindu festivals celebrated here are Nag Panchami, Pongal, Deepavali, Ram Leela and Vasanta Panchami. Deepavali or Diwali, the festival of lights is an important festival. It is celebrated in the mainland as well as in these islands but there is a lot of difference in celebrations here. Every house, irrespective of their religion or region, in the A&N Islands celebrate Deepavali by wearing new clothes, preparing and distributing sweets to near and dear ones. During evening hours, the houses are decorated with candles, series of lights and serial lamps and crackers are burst. Next to Deepavali, Maha Karthiakai festival in the honour of God Sri Murugan, the God of knowledge and courage, acquires importance. Apart from these festivals of the Hindus, Christians and Sikhs, there are also some important festivals which are celebrated among other communities living in these islands. They are — Jains celebrate the birthday of Lord Parasnath and Mahaveer; Buddhists celebrate Buddha Jayanti, and the Muslims celebrate Muharram, Ramzan, Bakri Eid etc. in which all participate with great enthusiasm.

5

Educational Fascinations

Introduction

People go from one place to another not only for enjoyment or to spend holidays, they even go for educational purposes. Tours and travels started to extend its scope to almost all fields/areas. It is the advantage of a particular place to attract people from various parts of the country and even the world due to its speciality. Andaman and Nicobar Islands is the best example for such attraction. Persons do visit this Green Paradise for educational purposes too.

Educational Purpose

Educational purpose means the purpose of visiting the place with a view to collect data on the subject matter of these islands. This is to study the situation, activities, growth factor, socio-economic development, to explore the possibility to set up of any venture, to conduct any research work etc. on Andaman and Nicobar Islands. In this territory, there are a lot of areas to attract people on special advantage of educational purposes possessed by each part of the economy. Such persons include the following:

1. Students
2. Scholars
3. Priests of various religions
4. Government officials in the name of delegates
5. Estimate committees
6. Study committees
7. Others (include entrepreneurs)

Students

This is a very important group. This group consists of school, college and university students and is the primary economic group. They are tomorrow's administrators. It is possible only if they go for better education. Education means knowledge. Andaman and Nicobar Islands is also one of the best places from where the knowledge can be acquired. Historical importance and resources available in the islands is the granary for the students. To give a broad vision, and enhance positive thinking, students should be brought to these islands and shown the socio-cultural day-to-day activities of the local populace. They should be taken to different places of historical importance like Cellular Jail and told about the history of freedom struggle. All students should make a study tour to these islands for educational knowledge.

Scholars

This is the second important economic group consisting of all research scholars of M. Phil, Ph.D. and D. Lit, D.Sc. projects, officers of research institutions etc. A scholar means a person who is actively involved in doing any type of research after finishing his schooling. He/She goes to a particular place with a view to collect information and after collection of such information, it is analysed, interpreted, compared, to arrive at new innovation and invention. In Andaman and Nicobar Islands, it can be said that developmental activities have not yet been started though these islands have been gifted with lot of natural resources. But none of them is fully exploited and majority of them is yet to be thought of. Lot of resources need to be exploited. Proper studies are to be conducted by disciplined and dedicated scholars to benefit the society at large.

This resourceful paradise extends its arms to welcome scholars from different parts of mainland with a lot of problem areas on which detailed research could be conducted. There are countries with lesser extent, areas and resources but more population, without sea-water but they stand on their legs with consistent good economic growth by challenging other developing countries and even some of the developed countries too. Research areas open for scholars may be categorised as:

1. Identification of the resources
2. Prospects of the marine wealth
3. Cost benefit analysis of education including higher education
4. Prospects of Tourism in Andaman and Nicobar Islands
5. Possibilities of increasing production (Agricultural Industries)
6. Possibilities of increasing the entrepreneurial development
7. Teaching and training for the administrators
8. Training for the head of the institutions
9. Possibilities of developing rural areas
10. Problems of tribals
11. Possibilities of operating air services
12. Possibilities for quality management
13. Possibilities for quality administration
14. Possibilities for increasing status of women
15. Possibilities starting industrial units in rural areas
16. Possibilities of teaching morality to government employees
17. Problems of Andaman Indians

18. Possibilities of removing ignorance
19. Possibilities of increasing awareness about AIDS and allied health issues
20. Possibilities of human resource development
21. Possibilities of increasing natural income; and the like.

Priests

This group consists of all religious heads or the religiously important people. Generally, they fall under the non-economic group. However, by taking the socio-cultural aspects into consideration, these gurus/heads of religions are considered the most important part in the society from a positive angle. When the two join their hands for their life, when any issue comes to the ground related to the religion, and when the position or situation comes, if such priests are important, then their visits to these islands are highly required. Hence, it has educational importance. Andaman and Nicobar Islands is an example of national integration of high degree. So, the style of life of the integrated people, the intrinsic characteristic, their movements, their way of success in their lives, their biological needs, wants, their economics of life etc. are to be studied. After the study is over, the findings are to be discussed with academicians to weed the unwanted issues. Then they can be implemented with government support. This educational importance will have high value to keep and promote peace. Such kind of work is to be carried out by priests who are really working for the spread of peace. For this big work and dedicated educational submission, Andaman and Nicobar Islands is the only suitable place.

Estimate Committees

This group is a non-economic group. Because, all expenses of this group are borne by the government only. It consists of elected politicians for the assemblies or the Parliament. They visit in-groups, stay in-groups, discuss in-groups, go around in-groups, and leave in-groups. They visit these islands only on certain job of estimation. Generally, these committees will not go to any place of problem. They discuss everything with the related officers and officials at higher levels in closed door meetings. But there are some dedicated committees, which will not be satisfied with the voice of the officers. So, they go on the spot and do their job. The estimate committees will do investigation, inspection, vouching, and verification etc. For any type of project to be introduced and implemented in India, the test estimate is an essential step in the process. Andaman and Nicobar Islands is the best and suitable place for such test estimates since it is mini-India. Hence, these islands have educational fascinations.

For all such groups of economic as well as non-economic importance, certain basic information about Andaman and Nicobar Islands is certainly necessary as Educational fascinations. These may not be fully needed but atleast to some extent of initiating their thinking processes. Such information is given below:

a. Educational Institutions

b. Population

d. Resources

e. Economy, Commerce and Industry

Educational Institutions

Education plays a very vital role in the process of human resource development. Number of educational institutions, namely schools, colleges, and institutions etc. has been increasing significantly. The tourism industry has a close positive correlation with the increase in number of educational institutions. What I want to say is that education is one of the aspects of the social system and that too an important organ of the social system. For the increase of educational institutions, tourism growth is not the only reason but that is one of the reasons/causes. But the growth of tourism industry compelled the administration to go for a separate course and as a result BTTM course was started. The course has now been renamed as BBA Tourism in JNRM Port Blair in the year 1999 and large numbers of applications for admission are evidence to its popularity. More number of students are doing Diploma courses in Tourism,

Courses for Tourist Guide etc. Though not all tourists are interested in educational institutions, some are interested to visit the higher educational institutions and meet professors, and associate professors and students depending upon their level of education.

In this territory there are only two colleges, one is Jawaharlal Nehru Government College in Port Blair City and the other one is Mahatma Gandhi Government Collage in Mayabunder. These two colleges offer arts, science and commerce courses at degree and Post Graduate levels. Besides these two colleges, one more specialized college namely Govt. B.Ed. College is in Port Blair which offers only B.Ed course for limited seats. The literacy rate of A&N Islands is — Male 78.99%, female 65.46% and overall 73.02% as per the 1991 census whereas the same in Port Blair city is 86.59%, 75.08% and 81.69% respectively. There are about 340 educational institutions in A&N Islands, including about 70 institutions in Nicobar Islands. The following table shows the growth of educational institutions due to the growth of tourism.

Table : 5.1
Growth of Educational Institutions

Sl. No.	Year	Institutions In Nos.	Change
01	1970	104	—
02	1975	217	Positive
03	1980	243	Positive
04	1985	284	Positive
05	1990	321	Positive
06	1995	341	Positive
07	2000	361	Positive

Source : Compiled from the Basic Statistics, A&N Administration, Rajavel, 1990

Presently, at school level, there are 188 primary schools, 43 middle schools, and 36 secondary schools and 42 senior

EDUCATIONAL FASCINATIONS & THE PERSONS INTERESTED

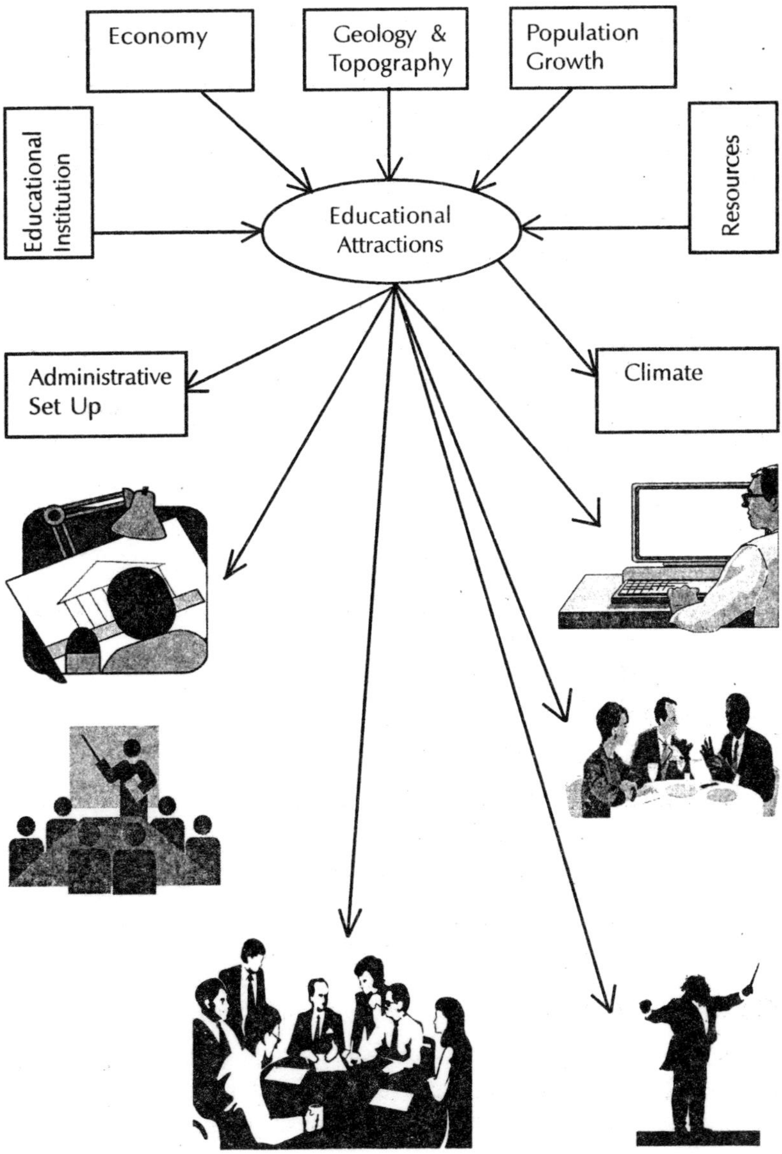

secondary schools are functioning. At college level, there are only three colleges, one for pursuing B.Ed. and two colleges for studying graduation. As far as technical education is concerned, there are only two Polytechnic Colleges and one ITI. In addition to all, one Teachers' Training Institute functions in this territory. The number of educational institutions in Andaman and Nicobar Islands is shown in the following table. Besides the students admitted in these colleges and institutes, some of them go for higher studies to the mainland. This is mainly for search in quality education, as they do not take admission in these colleges, for they want to prepare for the competitive examinations along with pursuing higher education.

Table : 5.2
Number of Educational Institutions in A&N Islands

Sl. No	Name of the Institutions	Number
1.	**At School Level**:	
	Primary Schools	188
	Middle Schools	43
	Secondary Schools	36
	Senior Secondary Schools	42
2.	**At College Level:**	
	B.Ed. College	01
	Degree Colleges	02
3.	At Technical Level:	
	Polytechnic Colleges	02
4.	**At Institute Level:**	
	Industrial Training Institute	01
	Teachers' Training Institute	01

Source : Basic Statistics, A&N Administration

Courses Offered

In school education, all courses namely, Arts, Science, and Commerce courses are offered in Tri-Lingual medium of instruction. As far as higher education is concerned, there are 15 courses namely – Commerce, Hindi, English, Bengali, History, Political Science, Geography, Home Science, Physics, Chemistry, Botany, Zoology, Tourism, Computer Science and Physical education are offered in the colleges. As far as technical education is concerned, diploma in civil engineering, mechanical engineering, electronic and electrical and communication engineering, fisheries engineering, fishing boat skippers and hotel reception and book keeping, house keeping and cookery are offered. Both the Polytechnics are in the Dollygunj, Port Blair Tehsil. Since, there is no professional college, specialised courses in these islands, the A&N Administration made arrangements for the students of these islands to continue their professional and specialised courses in the mainland. So, the Andaman and Nicobar Administration has been allotting seats in the mainland professional colleges and universities as per the guidelines of the Ministry of Human Resource Development and the Department of Education.

Population

The total population of A&N Islands as per 1991 census was 2, 80,661 constituting 1,54,346 males and 1,26,292 females. It formed only 0.03% of the total population of the country as a whole. The territory of A&N Islands was placed at 29th position by the size of population at the 1991 census. The following table indicates the changes in the population of A&N Islands since 1901.

Table : 5.3
Population of A&N Islands since 1901 (in No.)

Census Year	Andamans District	Nicobars District	Andamans and Nicobar Islands	Percentage of decadal variation
1901	18,138	6511	24,649	–
1911	17,641	8818	26,459	(+)7.34
1921	17,814	9272	27,086	(+)2.37
1931	19,223	10,240	29,463	(+)8.78

(Contd.)

1941	21,316	12,452	33,768	(+)14.61
1951	18,962	12,009	30,971	(–)8.28
1961	48,985	14,563	63,548	(+)105.19
1971	93,468	21,665	1,15,133	(+)81.17
1981	1,58,287	30,454	1,88,741	(+)63.93
1991	2,41,453	39,208	2,80,661	(+)48.70
2001	3,14,239	42,026	3,56,265	(+)26.94

Source : Census Report 1991, A&N Islands.

There was a slow and steady growth of population from 1911 to 1941, but there was a sudden decline in population in the decade 1941-51, both in the Andaman and in the Nicobar districts. The reason for the sudden decline might be due to the Second World War. The following table shows the population growth in A&N Islands from 1901:

Table : 5.4
Growth Rate of Population in A&N Islands

Decade	Percentage decadal variation in population		
	A&N Islands	**Andamans District**	**Nicobars District**
1901-11	(+) 7.34	(–) 2.74	(+) 35.43
1911-21	(+) 2.37	(+) 0.98	(+) 5.50
1921-31	(+) 8.78	(+) 7.91	(+) 10.44
1931-41	(+) 14.61	(+) 10.89	(+) 21.60
1941-51	(–) 8.28	(–) 11.04	(–) 3.56
1951-61	(+) 105.19	(+) 158.33	(+) 21.27
1961-71	(+) 81.17	(–) 90.81	(+) 48.77
1971-81	(+) 63.93	(-) 69.35	(+) 40.57
1981-91	(+) 48.70	(+) 52.54	(+) 28.74
1991-2001	(+) 26.94	(+) 30.15	(+) 7.19

Source : Basic Statistics and Census Report, 2001 Census Department, Port Blair

A remarkable decennial growth rate of 93% was recorded during the decade 1971-81 for A&N Islands as against the growth rate of 24.75% registered for the country as a whole. But during the next decadal year 1981-91, its growth rate was 48.7% in A&N Island as against the growth rate of 23% registered for the country as a whole. The districts of A&N Islands recorded a growth rate of 52.54% and 28.74% respectively, during the decade 1981-91. But comparatively, the growth of the population recorded fewer rates in the decade 1991-2001.

Literacy

As per 2001 census, the literacy rate in this territory is 81.18% consisting of male 86.07% and female 75.29%. The same literacy rate in urban areas is 86.48% consisting of male 90.35% and female 81.65% and in rural area, it is 78.55%, consisting of 83.90% and 72.23% respectively. As per the 1981 census, the literacy rate in this territory was 60.25% as compared to the all India average literacy rate of 36.23%. In the year 1991, the literacy rate of A&N Islands was 73.02% as compared to the all India average literacy rate of 52.11%, a considerable increase indeed. The relatively high percentage of literacy of the total population of these islands may be due to the increase in number of educational institutions in A&N Islands. These islands have a total of about 350 educational institutions, including two Govt. degree colleges, one B.Ed. degree college at Port Blair, and two Govt. Polytechnic institutions at Dollygunj village. The entire human resources of A&N Islands are spread over the inhabited islands.

Resources

Resources are the determinants of growth and development of a particular region or country as a whole. How fast the development and growth take place depends upon intellectuals and knowledge-oriented persons of the region. As far as these islands are concerned, they are fully blessed with plenty of resources. So exploiting resources is an important aspect for the development of the country. The resources of Andaman and Nicobar Islands are divided into five types:

1. Natural Resources
2. Water Resources
3. Marine Resources
4. Forest Resources
5. Plantation Resources

Natural Resources

No doubt, by God's grace the Islands have been bestowed with lot of natural resources. But for clarification purposes, the Natural Resources have been divided into four major groups namely Land Resources, Soil, Mineral and Scenic Beauty of these islands. The total land area of A&N Islands is 8293 sq. kms out of which the Andaman Group of Islands cover an area of 6340 sq. kms. and the Nicobar Group of Islands the remaining 1953 sq. kms. The available land resources of any country have a lasting effect on the economic life of man or nation because the production of raw materials depends greatly on the nature of landscapes. The available land resources are being utilized here. In the Andaman group of islands, the soil is generally fertile, supporting a varied type of forest vegetation, sandy alluvial soil, resulting from the deposition of fine material from the higher slopes in saline swamps and creeks, supports mangrove forests that fringe the islands in the sheltered coasts and Island creeks. The richer gray, brown and red soils, derived from the sand stones and serpentine rocks, support the major crops especially the forest crops. Soil depth differs from the slopes and shallow soils characterize the higher elevations. The soils have low moisture retention capacity. This supports rich forest or tree vegetation. Soils from calcareous, sand stones are deep and fertile with luxuriant growth of forests. In A&N Islands, the mineral resources are very limited. Chromium, Copper, Iron, Silver, Coal, Limestone, Oil and Gas are the mineral resources found in the A&N Islands. Three more wells, drilled on the same geological structure, proved dry. As per the Planning Commission, 1986 projected production of gas in Andaman and Nicobar Islands was 70 MMT in 1985-90 and 2230 to

4310 MMT in 1990-2000, where the projected production of oil is 1.22 to 1.45 MMT in 1990-2000.

Water Resources

No water means no life. The water resources are divided into two parts namely (a) Surface Water and (b) Ground Water. In any region, surface water resources (rivers, lakes) form the major sources of water for drinking, agricultural and industrial uses as well as for household needs. The streams are locally called as *nallahs,* meaning streams or small rivers. A&N Islands receive, on an average an annual rainfall of a little more than 300 mm. Besides the rainfall, the other sources of water are the surface water and ground water, which are the direct result of the rainfall received by the area itself. There is no lake or tank in these islands, except the Thilthaman tank which is situated in the heart of Port Blair City. During the rainy season, the (nallahs) streams are full of water and scarcity of water occurs only for four months. Even in the rainy season, scarcity of water for industrial activities is there in almost all the islands since there is no dam in these islands except the one named Dhannikari Dam in Port Blair.

The geography of A&N Islands is such that there are difficulties in the development of ground water resources. Saline aquifers (the interior rock zones having water) are encountered at shallow depths. The Central Ground Water Board (CGWB) has undertaken a systematic hydrological survey conducted by the CGWB and 11 promising sites bearing fresh water were pin-pointed in the South Andaman Islands. In some places, CGWB has succeeded in drilling tube wells. The well, dug in the God Alaikaddal Ayyanar campus with medium depth, gives very good drinking water. People of the surrounding areas are taking water from the well. The optimum exploitation of the land and meeting the basic human needs call for the proper planning and management of the Islands' water resources.

Forest Resources

The forests of A&N Islands are unique in character and possess enormous biological diversity. Of the 2,200 rare species of trees found in A&N Islands, about 200 species (10%) are endemic to these islands, but are found in Malaysia, Burma, Indonesia and Polynesian islands. The forests form one of the most important natural resources of a region. A&N Islands abound in forest wealth. The forests of A&N Islands provide adequate variety and quantity of trees. Some high quality hard wood trees, which are scarce or not seen in the mainland, are found in these islands in abundance. The Padauk trees, whose value as raw material for furniture is invaluable, are common in these islands. The forest area of this territory is 7,171 sq. kms. which is about 86% of the total lànd area of A&N Islands. Of reserve forests and 17 sq. kms. of protected forests and 4,112 sq. kms. for proposed reserve forests.

Plantation Resources

Next to Forest Resources, another man-made resources with the Natural Resources are the Plantation Resources. Systematic planning in Plantation Resources itself will make the region very rich. The plantation resources of A&N Islands include coconut, arecanut, rubber, red oil palm and other plantations like cashew nut, nutmeg, cinnamon etc. The location of these islands in the tropical belt and the high amount of rainfall provide favourable conditions for the natural growth of coconut plants. The area under coconut cultivation in these islands is about 22,000 hectares with a production of about 7.3 crores of nuts per annum. Nearly 2,020 hectares of A&N Islands are under areca-nut plantation and these plantations have a production of about 3,030 tons per annum. The Nicobar Group of Islands accounts for the bulk of the areas as well as the production. As far as rubber is concerned, the Rubber Board made an assessment in the year 1959 that about 4,000 hectares in Katchal, 1200 hectares in Rutland and about 2,400 hectares in Great Nicobar could be brought under rubber plantation. The soils as well as the agro-climatic conditions in the territory, particularly in the Nicobar Group of Islands, are suitable for the introduction of rubber plantation on a large-scale. At present, rubber plantation has been taken up in the South Andaman Group of Islands and

Katchal Islands of the Nicobar Group of Islands. In South Andaman, plantations were raised on revenue lands whereas in Katchal Island, the forest lands were utilized for this purpose. Latex, a product from the rubber plantations is tapped. Next to rubber, red palm oil is another important plantation. The Forest Department initiated, on an experimental basis, red palm oil cultivation in Little Andaman in 1975 and covered an area of 2,400 hectares. The area was however, restricted to 200 hectares only under instructions from the Government of India pending study with regard to the effect of red palm oil plantations on the environment and ecology of these islands. The red palm oil plantation involves clear felling of the rain forests. Pepper, cloves and cashew nuts are showing encouraging results.

Marine Resources

The Andaman and Nicobar Islands is very rich in marine resources. The apprehension of foreign vessels, which are coming in to our coastal area to explore the marine wealth proves the evidence of richness of marine resources. The deep sea around A&N Islands, the numerous inlets, bays and creeks are the abode of marine resources. The marine resources of A&N Islands may broadly be divided into two groups as fish and shell. This clearly indicates that there exists a vast scope for the development, exploitation and utilization of the fish resources of these islands. The rocky bottom has great potential for Percoid fishes (Porches an item of commercial importance, found in plenty in shallow waters around the main islands, is the Sea slug or Beach-de-mer (Holothurians). Out of nearly 40 species available, six species are of high commercial value which could yield substantial foreign exchange. A&N Islands is an abode of innumerable species of shells of various shapes and colours. The shells are used as raw materials in the shell handicraft industrial units, which is a growing, sector. Besides the shells, Five finger Chanks, Sacred Chanks, Pearly Oysters, Mussels, Clams, Cowries and numerous other varieties of high value and gastropod shells are found all along the shores.

Economy

The economy of A&N Islands consists of agriculture, trade, commerce and industry. At present, very little quantity of paddy, sugarcane, banana, sweet potato, papaya, rabi pulses and vegetables are cultivated. Among the Andaman cash crops, namely cashew nut, coconut, arecaunut are grown. Some other vegetables like tomato, potato, cabbage, onion, cauliflower, beans, carrot, green chilies etc. are brought from the mainland. As far as the trade and commerce is concerned, all types of trade are dominated by Tamilians and Punjabis. Though the wholesale and retail trades are common, the special type of trade namely "Govt. Order Supply" is very famous in these islands. As far as the industry is concerned, all types of industries are found in A&N Islands.

Commerce and Industry

Commercial and industrial development of A&N Islands plays an important role in the growth of tourism industry. Commercial and industrial units are the basis for shopping which forms an important activity of tourists in these islands. Though the units are scattered over the inhabited islands, majority of the units are located in Port Blair City. There are 892 shops and commercial establishments, 105 restaurants and 1,100 industrial units, functioning in these islands in order to serve and satisfy the tourists. The Port Blair City is very famous for its variety of items particularly the handicrafts shell-made items. Moreover, the prospects for such units in these islands are more. The present important trade centres are Aberdeen Bazaar, Diglipur, Junglighat, Middle Point, Bambooflat, Ferrargunj, Rangat, Mayabunder, and Campbell Bay etc.

Administrative Setup

A&N Islands, being a Union Territory, is under the direct rule of the President of India through the Lt. Governor as the Administrator. He is assisted by the Chief Secretary, Secretary (Planning)-cum-Development Commissioner, Finance Secretary-cum-Chief Pay and Accounts Officer, Judicial Secretary, Secretary

Shipping and Transport and Secretary to Lt. Governor. The A&N Administration continues to conduct its business in 19 major departments namely, Forest, Police, Public Works, Marine, Civil Supply, Transport, Agriculture, Animal Husbandry, Fisheries, Co-operative, Industries, Education, Medical and Public Health, Revenue, Justice, Electricity, Labour, Rehabilitation and Pay and Accounts. Besides, there are also a number of Central Government Departments. These are Andaman Harbour Works, Field Publicity Unit of the Ministry of Information and Broadcasting, Anthropological Survey of India, Lighthouses and Lightships Department, P and T Department, Zoological Survey of India, Botanical Survey of India, Meteorological Department, etc. in A&N Islands. Principal Chief Conservator of Forests and the Chief Engineer, APWD are functioning as Ex-Officio Secretaries to the Administration. Pradesh Council was constituted for A&N Islands on 20-6-81 on the pattern of the erstwhile Arunachal Pradesh Council, having functions of advisory nature. The Council consists of an administrator and has 29 members.

6

Places & Natural Fascinations

Introduction

Fascinations, Tourists both economic and non-economic tourists, Informational fascinations, Historical fascinations, Social and Cultural fascinations, Educational fascinations, Population fascinations, Tribal Population – Jarawas, Great Andamanese, Onges, Sentinalese, Nicobarese, Shompens etc. have been discussed in the previous chapters. This chapter concentrates on the Natural fascinations and the Places fascinations. A brief account is given on Natural Resources and on the different places of Andaman and Nicobar Islands.

Natural Fascinations

This is the real asset of any country/tourist destination and it requires no investment. Natural fascinations are pollution-free fascinations, which attract tourists in plenty to these islands. The geology and topography of A&N Islands itself are the most beautiful fascinations. The natural fascinations of these islands are divided into three types as mentioned above. They are discussed below:

1. Climate

2. Scenic Beauty
3. Flora and Fauna
4. Peaceful Place
5. Ship Journey
6. Places of Interest

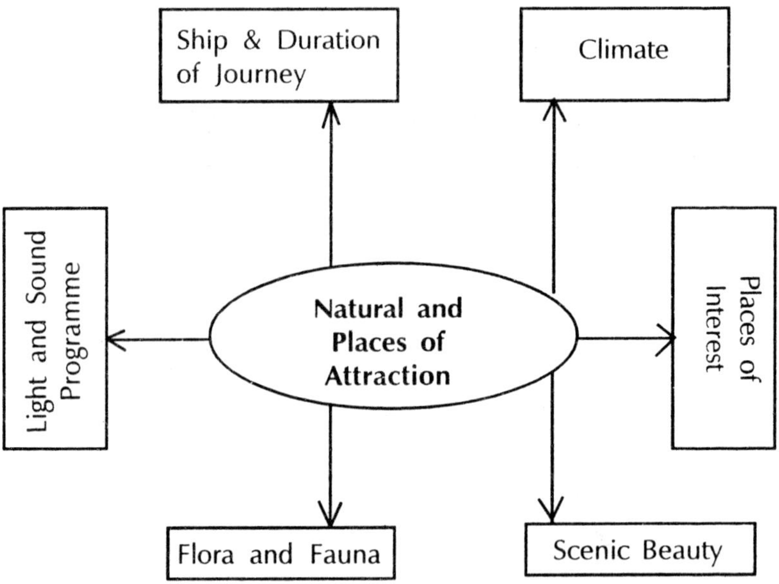

PLACES AND NATURAL FASCINATIONS

Climate

Travel and tourism is always based on weather and climate. Some like the cold climate, some the sunny climate and others warm climate. The climate suitable for one may not be suitable for another. The climate that is pleasant for one may not be pleasant for others. So climate is a factor that vitally affects tourism industry particularly in A&N Islands. Foreigners always like the sunny climate and some Indians like rainy and majority of them always like the cloudy climate. Hence, the climate of these islands always attracts tourists. Tourists can visit these islands in any season. But the best climate/season to visit the A&N Islands is from October to May. Then, from mid-October, northeast monsoon starts and continues till mid-December. When compared to southwest monsoon, northeast monsoon brings less rain. Foreign tourists like this climate and during this season/climate, the foreigners enjoy sun bathing on the sea-shore before going into the sea for a bath.

Of course, the Indian tourists also visit these islands during this climate. But the Indian tourists like the climate of cloudless sunlight, pleasant cool weather that prevails generally during the time between October and December. During this period, the tourists need not worry about rain; weather is very pleasant, cool breeze blows; sea remains very calm. Boat journey and ship journey are very convenient for tourists. Visiting inter islands by boat/ship during this season/climate is really wonderful. Tourists can witness the friendly (human brained) dolphins coming in groups and their beautiful swimming, jumping and entertaining the tourists. They accompany the boat to some distance.

Scenic Beauty

As is already explained that this territory is a God-gifted Paradise on the Blue surface. The scenic beauty of these islands is very marvelous and excellent for all types of tourists irrespective of religions, regions, age, liking and disliking, etc. The geology and topography are favourable for inducement and motivators of tourism. The hills, ups and downs of these Islands carry greater part of the scenic beauty. They have superlatives, peaks, and swifts, living species of plants and birds and animals like crabs. The golden sandy beaches, sparkling crystal clear sea, surrounded by beautiful mangrove forests, thick rain forests are nature's gift to these islands. Once a tourist goes into the forest (not reserved one) he will forget himself and enjoy the taste of peace. The underwater beauty is another scenic fascination. It is a separate world where one should come and enjoy.

So far, we have seen only the beauty on the earth and above the water level of these islands. But there is another world of joy in the underwater of Andaman and Nicobar Islands. The Coral reefs, under water marine life, multi-colour fishes, seaweeds plants and flowers make these islands a dreamland and the facility is provided by administration as a way to reach this dreamland. Tourists from different parts of the country enjoy the scenic beauty of the lush green forests. The sunrise and sunset and moonrise and moonset is a treat to watch and convinces us to extend our stay further.

Creeks and sanctuaries also share the scenic beauty of any place and our Andaman and Nicobar Islands stands first, if any one ranks it. So they also share the responsibility of attracting tourists to this Green Paradise. Travelling through the creeks, surrounded by the thick mangrove forests, makes the tourists happy and cheerful. Some tourists may even be inspired to write a poem, story etc. These creeks are resourceful to film producers since they are suitably located for film shooting. The scenic view from one end to another with some island/islands as background has its own beauty, which cannot be seen elsewhere in the world. As a resource, this scenic resource (Natural Resource) has not at all been touched for any commercially productive purposes. This area is open to researchers as well. The important creeks in A&N Islands are given in the table:

Table : 6.1
The Important Creeks

Sl. No.	Name of the important Creeks	Location
01	Wright Myo	South Andaman
02	Baratang	South Andaman
03	Uttara	Middle Andaman
04	Yeratta	Middle Andaman
05	Kalighat	North Andaman
06	Parangara	North Andaman

Sources : Basic Statistics, A&N Administration

Next to the creeks, sanctuaries draw a lot of tourists. Sanctuaries are vital for preservation of its fragile eco-system. In A&N Islands there are 94 sanctuaries. Some sanctuaries are inhabited and the others are uninhabited. The songs of different birds, beauty of their structure and the way of life which can be seen in these sanctuaries and is really worth watching. In particular, tourists get excellent scenic beauty from some particular spots. Starting from the Cellular Jail, top terraces of the wing which is adjacent to the hospital offer a good scenic view. All India Radio (protected area) is situated in Delanipur village. From the car parking place inside the AIR, the tourists can see the sea, hills, forests, trees, islands, fascinating landscape, plantation etc. Likewise view from Mount Harriet, Carbine's Cove, Tower Hill, Police Line Hill, North Bay light house, from Car Nicobar, Nancowry and Chowra are really worth watching.

Flora and Fauna

Everything created by God has its own importance. From a small ant to a big elephant, a small rose plant to a big tree, *chiddia* to peacock and from monkey to man have their roles assigned by God. "Flora and Fauna" is one of the very valuable and tangible factors which determine the importance of every place. Flora and fauna contain a lot of importance namely, peace importance, medical importance, educational importance, value importance, economic importance, research importance, beauty importance, trade importance, commerce importance and tourism importance. So they too have a different role to play in the development of tourism industry. Since Andaman and Nicobar Islands possesses natural fascinations drawing the attention of mainlanders both domestic and foreign, the flora and fauna of these islands adds more horse power to natural fascinations.

Forests occupy about 86 % (7,144 sq. kms.) of the land area in A&N Island. Forests of A&N Islands are unique in character and possess enormous biological diversity. Out of 15,000 flowering plants in India, 2,200 species are found in this lush green paradise, of which 200 species (about 10%) are endemic in these islands and 1,300 species are not found in the mainland of India. At present, about 40 species are harvested for commercial purposes. Almost all types of flowers are planted in each and every park situated in different places of the Islands.

As far as the fauna in this Green Paradise is concerned, about 55 species of mammals and 255 species of birds have been recorded in these islands. This is out of 350 species of mammals and 1,200 species of birds found in India. Some of the endemic, endangered species of mammals include the Nicobar crabs, Andaman wild pig and few species of rodents and bats. The avifauna is spectacular with a number of endemic endangered species, such as the Andaman Teal, Narcondum Hornbill, Nicobar Megapode, Nicobar pigeon etc. There is a large influx of migrant coastal and shallow water sea birds. Many new species of birds and animals have been introduced namely spotted deer, barking deer, feral goats and feral elephants, which attract the visitors.

Floristically, the forests have been classified into the following types (H G Champion and S K Seth): 1) Giant Ever Green Forests, 2) Andaman Tropical Ever Green Forests, 3) Southern Hill top tropical Ever Green Forests, 4) Andaman Semi-Ever Green Forests, 5) Andaman Moist Deciduous Forests, 6) Cane Brakes, 7) Bamboo Brakes, 8) Littoral Forests, and 9) Tidal Swamp Forests. Timber is available in plenty in the above forests which is valuable and is in a vast variety.

Peaceful Place

Andaman and Nicobar Islands, due to its location, is said to be in the most remote part of India. But it is a peaceful place. No doubt, it is the solid paradise in green colour on the blue surface. Here, people of different religions from different regions and various states of the country are living unitedly without any problem and difference of opinion. So, the question of communal disturbances is far from one's normal thinking. Moreover, this resourceful paradise is free from the so-called poisonous pollution. Here, in this golden paradise, there is no water pollution and hence there is no pollution of any kind.

Hence, these islands are the suitable place for the people who really want to enjoy their life with their families too.

Natural scenic beauty, soft touching sea breeze, happy feeling inducers of the general weather, love and life motivating flora and fauna, a new cultural life of the people of these islands, are the fascinations which will take the peace-lovers to an entirely different world of supreme sublimity. One more addition is to be mentioned here is that the tourists (domestic) can move around the permitted places at any time without any fear. The people of these islands including the officers and the policemen are very helpful to visitors of these islands. Keeping enough space for all exceptions, local people mingle with visitors as per their tradition.

There are places in these islands where one can go, sit and start writing stories, and songs on nature, on his lover, place etc. This is a beautiful place for meditation also. Of course, the spots need to be developed. Sometimes people go to a hill station to spend their holidays. By knowing the season, they can come to this paradise and enjoy the brimming beauty of these islands. As majority of tourists don't have proper information about the season of this green paradise they cannot plan a visit here. The following table will give you the information about the position of the season. This information has been collected personally out of practical experiences since the last three years. So, if one comes to these islands to enjoy a peaceful holiday, certainly he will go back with a lot of satisfaction.

Table : 6.2
Position of the Tourist Season

Sl. No	Month	Qualitative Scale
01.	January Full	Excellent
02.	February Full	Excellent
03.	March Full	Excellent
04.	April Full	Excellent

(Contd.)

	Qualitative Scale	
05.	May upto 15th	Excellent
06.	May from 16 to 31st	Good
07.	June upto 15th	Good
08.	June from 16th to 30th	Average
09.	July	Not Good
10.	August	Not Good
11.	September	Not Good
12.	October upto 15th	Average
13.	October from 16th to 30th	Good
14.	Novernber	Excellent
15.	December upto 20th	Good
16.	December from 20th to 31st	Excellent

Source: Primary Data — Personal Experience

The scenic beauty emerges like a beautiful green oasis in the Bay of Bengal. A most hospitable and cosmopolitan society, free from rigidity of caste, creed and religion, projecting Indian culture, unity in diversity is the A&N Islands, today. The undulating terrain, the inter-play of land, sea and creeks, the bright white trips of sea beaches that the blue bays, the rich tropical forests fringed by bright green mangroves, all combine to enhance the scenic value of the Islands in a way not to be found anywhere else in the country.

About Ship Journey

For all tourists the ship journey may be the first experience. This is to be really enjoyed. The best season for the ship journey is from October to mid-December and from mid-January to April end. During this period the sea will be calm. Sitting on the deck/ terrace (Top floor of the ship-open space) with a glass of cold drinks and a plate of Kaaram (mixture), sipping once with an interval of 3-4 minutes, seeing the catchy blue water in a pleasant wind and weather, is really a happy, and cheerful feeling which cannot be equalized with and by anything. Sunrise and sunset are the marvelous scenes which one should not miss watching.

The human brained fish called dolphins, and flying fishes are always visible and show their presence in their own way by jumping up and down, flying etc., will make the travellers stay in the ship itself. Sitting inside the cabin one can also enjoy all such scenes by keeping the window open. Cinema, tambolas, pictures etc. are also arranged inside the ships by the welfare officer of the ships with a view to provide pleasant journey and entertainment. Medical, shop, bar, canteens etc., are other facilities provided on the ship. Some tourists/travellers may have mild sea-sickness, which can be totally avoided. The travellers who feel a vomiting sensation can chew lemon. So travellers may carry the following eatables with them for full enjoyment. The quantity of eatables given in table is for one journey for one person for three days.

Table : 6.3
Eatables to be Carried During Ship Journey

S.No.	Name of the items	Quantity for one person
1.	Avomine Tablets	3 Nos.
2.	Lemon/Ginger/Mango Pickle	100 grams.
3.	Bread	2 Pkts.
4.	Jam	50 grams.
5.	Heavy Kaaram (Mixture)	250 grams
6.	Saltea biscuits	2 Pkts.
7.	Lemon Fruit	3 Nos.
8.	Orange or apple	3 Nos.

Source : Primary data — personal experience

For the purpose of tourists, the information about the level of sea-sickness during various months is given in the table. From this table it is very clear that the best season for tourism in these islands starts from October 15th to May 15th. Variations in the level of seasickness felt over the year are given in the table:

Table : 6.4
Level of Sickness

S.No	Month	Level of Sea-Sickness			
		More	Certainly	Slight	Not at all
1.	January	-	-	-	✓
2.	February	-	-	-	✓
3.	March	-	-	-	✓
4.	April	-	-	-	✓
5.	May upto 15th	-	-	-	✓
6.	May upto 31st	-	-	✓	-
7.	June upto 15th	-	-	✓	-
8.	June upto 30th	-	✓	-	-
9.	July	✓	-	-	-
10.	August	✓	-	-	-
11.	September	✓	-	-	-
12.	October upto 15th	-	✓	-	-
13.	October upto 30th	-	-	✓	-
14.	November	-	-	-	✓
15.	December upto 20th	-	-	✓	✓
16.	December upto 31st	-	-	-	✓

Source : Own Experience — Primary Data – Rajavel-1998

Duration of Journey

As per the statistics of the authorities, the ships are expected to reach the destination within 54 hrs., but practically the ship journey takes and consumes 3 nights and 2 days or 3 days and 2 nights depending upon the weather conditions adverse and/ or favourable. If weather conditions are favourable the ship reaches the destinations even before the scheduled time otherwise it takes even more than 5 days. But during the tourist season, the ships reach the destinations as per the scheduled time.

Attractive Places (Places of Interest)

Different important places and their importance are the other set of fascinations of the region. One more point to be noted here is that tourists never like to stay at one place even if they go for tour or picnic. After reaching a particular destination, they visit other interesting destinations too. Even if there is a small level of importance, tourists would like to go and see that place. These Islands have a lot of such interesting places. They are listed below in two sections:

Section I

1. Andaman Water Sports Complex
2. Anthropological Museum
3. Cellular Jail
4. Chatham Saw Mill
5. Children's Traffic Park
6. Cottage Industries Emporium
7. Fisheries Museum
8. Gandhi Park
9. Gymkhana Ground
10. Mahatma Gandhi National Marine Park (Jolly Bouy and Red Skin)
11. Marina Park
12. Mini Zoo
13. Samundrica
14. Wandoor Beach

Section II

1. Barren Island
2. Chidiyatappu
3. Cinque Island
4. Corbyn's Cove
5. Diglipur

6. Havelock
7. Long Island
8. Madhuban
9. Mayabunder
10. Mount Harriet
11. Neil Island
12. Port Blair City
13. Rangat
14. Ross Island
15. Shippighat
16. Viper Island

Section I

Andaman Water Sports Complex (AWSC)

This place is in Port Blair City. It is newly developed and attracts a large number of local people and tourists, both domestic and foreign every day. Generally the water sports complex is full of tourists during the day time as well as evenings though the rush is more during the evening hours. AWSC is situated in Aberdeen Jetty, just one km. from Port Blair Bus Terminus. Walking around this AWSC gives a pleasant feeling, sweet breeze, a wonderful sight of glittering waves etc. to the tourists. This is a unique sports complex in India and one of its own kind. In the AWSC, the tourists are given the facilities for safe water sports and adventure water sports. The safe water sports facilities include Rowing Boats, Paddle Boats, Kayaks, Aqua-cycle, Aqua-glide, Bumper Boats, the Gemini Boats, Para-Sailing, Sail Boats, Wind-Surfacing, Speed Boats, Glass Bottom Boats etc. The Complex also has a saline water swimming pool, Food Plaza, Change Room, Toilet and Children Traffic Park etc. and is open all days. Timings for the Safe Water Sports are 8 am to 8 pm. and for Adventure Water Sports 8 am to 5 pm. Tourists and local people enjoy playing water sports here as they are able to go very near the historically important island, named Ross Island.

Anthropological Museum

Previously it was situated at a distance of 1.25 kms. from Port Blair Bus Terminus on Haddo via Phoenix Bay route. But now it is situated in the heart of the Port Blair City. It is just at a walkable distance from anywhere in the Port Blair City. This museum displays the tools, instruments, models and habitats of the tribals named Great Andamanese, Jarawas, Sentinalese, Onges, Nicobarese and Shompens. The tribals' arts and handicrafts are very attractive and induce the tourists to think seriously about the art and culture of the tribals. This display provides rare opportunity to the Indian tourists as well as foreign tourists to compare today's space age with the stone-age and how the humans travelled from the stone-age to space. Such tribal arts are giving some basic ideas to our present day artisans to produce various handicrafts. The museum is open to tourists on all days. Another important point to be noted is that this Museum is surrounded by the Indian Airlines Booking Office, Telephone Bhavan, Head Post Office, Head Telegraphic Office, Secretariat, Hotels, Raj Niwas, Pay and Accounts Office, Deputy Commissioner's Office, Tagore College of Education and the Courts.

Cellular Jail

This is situated in Port Blair City. The Cellular Jail is a National Memorial. It is located just two kms. from the Port Blair Bus Terminus. One can come here even by walk. If you take an auto it will cost Rs.10 from the Bus Terminus. It is the most important landmark of Port Blair and even India. This is known as Bastille of India and relic of bygone years where India's freedom fighters were incarcerated. The Cellular Jail brings back to the mind of the tourist "a saga of struggle for emancipation of people kept in bondage by the alien power". Every molecule of the wall and floor has a harrowing tale to tell. Now the Cellular Jail has been declared as a national monument since 11th Feb, 1979. The saga of this heroic struggle is now brought alive in a Moving son-at Lumiere (sound and light show). The Department of Tourism runs this show based on the history of this island and jail as if it is told by the oldest "peepal tree", still standing inside the Jail. The Cellular Jail has now become the place of pilgrimage for all Indian and the educated freedom loving people etc. Timings to go around the Cellular Jail during all days are between 9 am and 5 pm with a lunch break between 12 noon and 1 pm. There is ever increasing tourist traffic to the National Memorial. For further details about the Cellular Jail please see the chapter in the historical fascinations. List of freedom fighters who have been hanged by British Jailers is also given.

Chatham Saw Mill

The Chatham Saw Mill is one of the largest saw mills in Asia. This is situated in Chatham Island, about 4 kms from Port Blair Bus Terminus. It is a separate island connected with Port Blair by road on bridge. This mill has two biggest cranes called EOT cranes which are used for both stacking and feeding. Wood workshop of this mill is worth visiting. This saw mill functions as a store-house of timber like Padauk, Gurjan, Marble, Satine wood etc. This Chatham Island has the second largest wharf of these islands and here big ships from the mainland are berthed.

Children's Traffic Park

This is situated in the Port Blair City, just behind the Marina Park. The Children Traffic Park is a newly erected park and is very beautiful looking. All traffic rules are written on the wall in bold pictures. All features of the traffic are written, drawn and constructed in the Park. The pillars with different traffic lights in small sizes, speed breakers, small milestones, cemented roads etc. are beautifully constructed. At present the children of domestic tourists and locals practice, bicycle, tri-cycle, baby motor etc. inside the park. All vehicles for children are available for hire. The Tourism Department manages this park. They charge Re.1 per head as entry fee and Rs.2 per vehicle as hire charge for the duration of an hour. This Children's Park is set up with a view to educate the young children about traffic rules.

Cottage Industries Emporium

The Cottage Industries Emporium is also situated in the Port Blair City. This is a government owned emporium. This emporium is in the Middle Point at a distance of about 2 kms. from Port Blair Bus Terminus, run by the A&N Administration through the Directorate of Industries. They function as a showroom and marketing place. All local handicrafts wood-made, shell-made, cane-made etc. are sold in the emporium. Tourists can buy their needs here even by placing orders at their own will. The prices are comparatively low. This emporium is always crowded with visitors, tourists, buyers' etc. Foreign tourists are very fond of shell items, wooden dancing dolls and wooden walking sticks. Pen stands, night lamps, necklace, table weight, and domestic tourists especially like shell calendar. Cottage Industries Emporium is open from 9 am to 5 pm on all working days. The local artisans keep their special products in the showroom for sale. By seeing the models, tourists place orders for the goods. Within a very short period, the artisans are able to supply the goods to tourists. Even non-economic tourists visit this place to admire the beauty of these products.

Fisheries Museum

Fisheries Museum is in Port Blair City and is situated in the Shadipur via JNRM (Government College) route. It is surrounded by Marina Park, Andaman Water Sports Complex, and Children's Traffic Park, within 1.5 kms. from Port Blair Bus Terminus. It exhibits species of marine life peculiar to the islands and found in the Indo-Pacific and Bay of Bengal. Over 350 species of marine life have been very carefully preserved in this Museum. Now a days even the local population (means the people who are living in Port Blair City) visit the museum. It gives an intellectual insight to both, the domestic and foreign tourists and the local people, particularly the student category about the nature and character of marine life found in A&N Islands and the marine wealth in these islands. At present it is called the Marine Museum. Tourists are allowed to visit the museum during the working hours, on all working days. The recent developments are that the young trade entrepreneurs have started displaying few varieties of shell-made items on pavements in such a way that the traffic is not affected. The tourists buy the items at cheaper rate from these vendors.

Gandhi Park

This is another beautiful and newly created park in Port Blair City at a distance of just one km. from Port Blair Bus Terminus. It is situated very near to Sri Vetrimalai Murugan Temple. This park is made on the bank of Thilthaman Water Tank (big pond). It can rightly be told that it is a full-fledged complete park because it has all the facilities including children's park, amusement park, entertainment park, deer park, water sports, nature walk, lake garden and a marvelous restaurant etc. Gandhi Park has been constructed with the Japanese Temple in the centre. Tourists enjoy the colourful lamps during evening hours.

In fact, the tourists visiting these islands do not return without visiting this park. Children are extremely happy when they play in the park. Since this park contains different items including boating facilities, visitors will never get bored. A baby electric train is also there. This park attracts children who are happy to come here and enjoy themselves. Even elders join in the fun. This park is full of tourists during evening hours particularly on Sundays and holidays. Another important point to be noted is that this park contains a beautiful restaurant in which often parties like dinner parties, tea parties and all functions including marriages are organised. This is open on all days.

Gymkhana Ground

This is a very big and famous play ground in Andaman and Nicobar Islands. This ground is situated just opposite the Marina Park and is within 1 km. from Port Blair Bus Terminus on Shadipur via J.N.R.M. route. The last part of the ground has a velodrome. The initial part of the ground consists of an international level standard swimming pool, which is a newly created facility. This ground also has a Stadium, Sports complex, and Velodrome, besides night play facilities in Netaji Stadium where all the functions, parade, festivals competitions, annual days, sports days of colleges and schools are celebrated. The Ground was used for organising the Andaman Trade Fair Festival and the Tourism Festival, though now a days it is organised in a separate place called Kamarajar Nagar.

Mahatma Gandhi Marine National Park (JollyBouy and Red Skin)

This Nature's Heaven attracts researchers and scientists for academic purposes. Foreign tourists are thrilled to see the beauty of this park. Mahatma Gandhi Marine National Park is a newly declared park. It is located 30 kms. from Port Blair on south west coast of the main South Andaman Island. It covers an area of 281.5 sq. kms. and is made up of open sea, creeks and 15 islands. Of the 15 islands, the most important are JollyBuoy and Red Skin which are open to tourists. The fringing type of coral reefs growing around these islands attracts tourists. More than 50 types of corals are found in JollyBuoy and Red skin islands. These two islands have beautiful and excellent sandy beach with crystal clear water.

Colourful fishes, variety of coral reef, fishes like clown fishes, butterfly fishes, surgeon fishes, angel fishes, parrot fishes, bat fishes, sea anemone fishes, tiger fishes, sea cucumber, special big prawn fish, etc. overwhelm the tourists with their beauty. Besides fishes, other marine lives found are star fish, sea lilly, feather star, giant clam shell, troches sea cucumber, sponges, sea anemones etc. Tourists can go upto Wandoor by bus from Port Blair Bus Terminus. From Wandoor Jetty, they have to avail boat transport facilities, provided by the Tourism Department, Andaman and Nicobar Administration and some private tour operators, to reach these islands. While going to these islands, tourists can enjoy the natural beauty of Mangrove forests along with creeks and magnificent tropical forest. JollyBuoy and Red Skin islands are fully resource with the fascinating coral reefs and rare underwater marine life like exotic varieties of beautifully coloured coral fishes. The sea transport operators offer beautiful glass bottom boats by which tourists can enjoy the beauty of under-water marine life.

Marina Park

This park is situated in Port Blair City within 1 km. from Port Blair Bus Terminus and on Shadipur via J.N.Govt. College route. This is a colourful park of national importance just in front of the Children's Traffic Park and is situated on the road. Shri Netaji Subhash Chandra Bose's statue is erected inside this park. This park has been extended with the Children's Park. Colourful flowers, beautiful looking garden, a small children park, a semi-canteen, illuminative lightings etc. are the special features of this park.

The management of the park has given a separate place with a semi-structured fence for rabbits. The antics of the little white creatures attract many child tourists who are thrilled to see these. The park is full of visitors during evening hours everyday. Tourists can go around at any time during the day. Recently a new restaurant has opened here where the tourists can enjoy the tasteful Biryani. Since this Park is connected with the Children's Traffic Park and Aberdeen Water Sports Complex with the Shri Netaji Subhash Chandra Bose statue and beautiful sea view, now a days it is regarded as place of pride of the Port Blair City.

Mini Zoo

This is actually an attraction for children of these islands. Here there is no chance of seeing wild animals or even some rare pet animals. The Mini Zoo fills up the gap and satisfies the wants of the local people, particularly the children. Mini Zoo is situated in Port Blair and is about 2.5 kms. from Port Blair on the Chatham route. Tourists are specially fascinated by the beautiful birds here. Some of them are Nicobar Pigeons, Emerald Dove, Megapode, Black Myanas, Imperial Pigeons, Parakeets, Andaman Cuckoos, Nicobar Cuckoos, Teals etc.

A group of deers with marvellous horns has been enchanting the tourists here. The salt-water crocodile-rearing farm is a special fascination too. Timing to visit this mini zoo is from 7 am to l2 noon and from l pm to 5 pm on all working days. Inside the zoo, the administration recently constructed a small children's play park with a rest-halt facilities. Tourists visiting this place spend an entire day here and relax.

Samundrica

It is situated 2 kms. from Port Blair Bus Terminus on Haddo via Delanipur route, just opposite the Andaman Teal House.

This is exactly like the Fisheries Museum with some added features, kept neat and clean. It is a self-descriptive museum. A good collection of literature is displayed on special wallboards (write-ups) and models are the special features of this Samundrica. A good collection of shells, corals, fishes and a few species of colourful fishes, snakes, anemone fishes, bones of dangerous fishes, drawings of different marine lives are displayed in the museum. This is run under supervision of the Defence authorities and is, therefore, called as a Naval Marine Museum. Tourists can witness a wide variety of shells and marine life in A&N Islands. The main purpose of the Samundrica Museum is to create awareness among the people on various aspects of oceanic environment. Tourists can enjoy their precious 2 hours usefully by going around this museum. Samundrica is open to tourists on all days during working hours except on Sundays and public holidays.

Wandoor Beach

Wandoor is another important place for people of all ages to go for pleasure. It is a beautiful place for diving, and swimming and is famous for holiday picnic. Next to Carbyn's Cove, this is a very suitable place for snorkeling. It offers a picturesque landscape and an ideal place for diving. Wandoor beach is the entrance to the famous Marine Park named as Mahatma Gandhi Marine National Park consisting of 15 islands of which the main Islands are JollyBuoy and Red Skin, the only islands open for tourists in the National Park. The Wandoor beach is situated in 30 kms. from Port Blair town on the West Coast of South Andaman. This is a beautiful sand beach attracting both domestic as well as the foreign tourists.

The students of local colleges, schools, institute etc. defence personnel, teachers, and office employees of the administration, all like to visit to this Wandoor beach. Transparent and crystal clear water with coral reef offers an exotic opportunity to observe interesting under water life. The visitors forget themselves as long as they are on the beach. This is an ideal place for fishing too. Wandoor has a beautiful guest house with a marvellous scenic beauty from all directions, run by the A&N Islands. Tourists and visitors can stay there after obtaining permission from the Forest department, i.e.' Chief Wildlife Warden, Port Blair. For food facilities, there are small hotels situated near the bus stop. The prices are comparatively low. Tender coconuts and other stall items are sold nearby the bus stand. This beach can be developed further in order to attract more tourists.

Section II

BARREN ISLAND

Barren Island is a geographically and geologically important island. It is situated at a distance of 135 kms. by sea and is an uninhabited island. Generally nobody is permitted, to go there by the administration. The reason is an active volcano and the only active volcano in India named 'Barren Island Volcano'. It erupted twice in the recent past, once in 1991 and again in 1994-95 after 177 years. This island is in about 3 kms. in diameter has a big crater of volcano, which rises abruptly from the sea, about half km. from the shore and is about 150 fathoms deep. At present, the volcano is dormant. Tourists cannot go to this island. However, with the permission of the Andaman and Nicobar Administration, one can go nearby for some academic purposes and as per the directions of the authorities.

CHIDIYATAPPU

This place is generally known as 'Bird Island'. In Hindi language 'Chidia' means 'small bird' and "tappu" means hill, highest place. All birds migrate to this place as a resort. Most of the species of birds found in A&N Island are found here. The Chidiyatappu is the southern-most tip of the South Andaman and is situated at a distance of 28 kms. from Port Blair Bus Terminus. By bus it takes an hour to reach here from the Port Blair Bus Terminus and 30 minutes by private transport. Chidiyatappu provides a panoramic view, scenic beauty, lush green view and lovable blue oceanic view. This is easily the most picturesque beach for picnics and fishing. The surrounding lush green mangroves and the abundance of birds add natural touch to the whole area which attracts the tourists. At present a large number of tourists and local visitors walk through the jungle to enjoy the nature's beauty.

This sand beach, like Carbyn's Cove beach, has transparent, clear water of the same level upto 0.5 kms. from the shore. Sitting under the shadow of the trees very near the beach and hearing the sweet songs of the 'singing chidias', twitter of swallows, screams of squirrels, coos of pigeons and cuckoos, talks and speeches of parrots and singing larks alongwith the pleasant breeze are the fascinations of this beach. One tends to forget himself/herself here. A beautiful sand beach is within 2.75 kms. from Chidiyatappu Bus Stop. This is situated in a place called "Munda Pahar". To reach the beach, tourists have to take an auto, taxi, car or jeep. There is no bus service so far. But many tourists trek it out. A fine road has been made between the Chidiyatappu Bus Stop upto this spot.

CINQUE ISLAND

This is situated 35 kms. from Port Blair and is declared as a sanctuary. This island too is an uninhabited one. Cinque Island is an enchanting one with rare corals and under-water marine life, a fine sandy beach and tropical rain forest. This beach is excellent for diving, snorkeling, sun-bath, sand-bath etc. and offers the lure of underwater corals ground and beautiful beach. Dolphins greet the visitors as if in cheerful welcome.

CARBYN'S COVE BEACH

No doubt the mainland beaches are big in size and distance. The sand contents will also be more. But island beaches are always small in size and small is always beautiful and so is the case of Andaman and Nicobar Islands too. All beaches in these islands are beautiful. Carbyn's Cove Beach is one of the most important beaches in this territory and can rightly be called as 'Kovalam' of A&N Islands. The coconut nursery in Carbyn's Cove is worth watching. The Agriculture Department has opened up a sales counter for tender coconuts at the beach. Every year on the night of Chaitra Pournami (Buddha Poornima), the beach brims up with tourists.

The Carbyn's Cove Beach provides a beautiful scenic view generally, marvellous sun-rise, moon-rise, etc. in particular. Tourists can enjoy the natural beauty of the A&N Islands. This beach is fully decorated with the sodium vapour lamps. This sandy beach is an ideal place for swimming. Foreign tourists enjoy their sun bath, moon bath, and star bath when there is no moon. They don't find any difference in day and night as long as they are in Carbyn's Cove beach. Domestic tourists spend maximum part of their stay in Carbyn's Cove.

This Beach is situated in Port Blair and is within 7 kms. from Port Blair Bus Terminus towards south-east direction. Carbyn's Cove Beach is one of the most beautiful picturesque sea beaches of A&N Islands, named after Reve. H.Corbyn, the Chaplain of the Settlement. Just in front of the beach, there is a hotel called Peerless Resort (previously named as Andaman Beach Resort), which provides quality food, water sports facilities including diving. One more restaurant namely 'The wave' provides open air bar facility. This is an excellent and eminent beach for picnic for employees, workers, businessmen, professionals like doctors, youth and students.

DIGLIPUR

It is a separate island and is in the North Andaman. It is an inhabited island. Socially this island is very important. The sea distance between Diglipur and Port Blair is 185 kms. Saddle peak, the highest point in Andaman and Nicobar Islands (732 mtrs) is near this Island. The nearby next headquarter is Mayabunder. There are boats between Mayabunder and Diglipur. The distance between Mayabunder and Diglipur is 28 kms. The total population of these islands is 42,880 with a growth rate of 80.67% over the census of 1991 (23,734). Diglipur has the rural status as per 2001 census. The settlers of this island are Bengalis, Malayalis, Tamilians and Telugus.

The main occupation of the population is cultivation of paddy, vegetable and fruits. Diglipur Island is looked upon as the "Granary of A&N Islands" (Rajavel 1990) and in particular it is famous for oranges. Kalipur sandy beach has been developed as a tourist complex. Tourists can reach the island by boat directly from Port Blair or from Aerial Bay or from Mayabunder. Otherwise, tourists can go upto Mayabunder by bus and from Mayabunder to Kalighat village by a small boat by crossing a creek, Mayabunder Kalighat creek which is the longest one. From Kalighat to Diglipur they can go by bus. Tourists can see sea crocodiles while crossing the creek. During Durga Pooja, different places of the Diglipur Island are illuminated with colourful lights and a number of temporary shops come up around these places. During Pooja time, the inter-islands tourists visit the Diglipur Island.

HAVELOCK

This island is at a distance of 57 kms. from Port Blair Phoenix Jetty connected by ferry service. It takes 5 hours to reach this island from Port Blair depending upon weather conditions. This island is named as "Havelock" after the famous Gen. Havelock of the first war of India's independence. Havelock is another important developing island and a very beautiful one. Economically too, the Havelock Island has been acquiring importance. With its lush green forests and sandy beaches this island is partly hilly and partly plain and is an inhabited one. The Havelock Island is very famous for vegetables as they are available at cheap rates. The wholesalers and agents of vegetables from different islands come here to purchase vegetables and sell in other islands, particularly at Port Blair.

The main occupation of the people of this island is cultivation of vegetables and fruits. The main feature of this island is that the land is very fertile; the beaches are natural, serene and unpolluted. Near the Jetty, the Tourism Department has constructed a beautiful accommodation called Yatri Niwas. Among the beaches, the most important one is Radha Nagar beach, which attracts lots of tourists, and is situated at a distance of about 10 kms. from Yatri Niwas. The Tourist Department has developed this beach with utmost care. It provides all facilities. Tourists can enjoy the antics of Dolphins, the marine life and other flying fishes etc., when they travel by ferry to this island. After enjoying the beauty of this island, tourists generally purchase vegetables and fruits from this island. A detailed study will help explore different ways and means to develop this island.

LONG ISLAND

Long Island is a small and beautiful inhabited island. Though the population is less, most of these people are employed in the Small Scale Industrial Unit. The Long Island has an important beautiful unpolluted natural sandy beach called Lalaji Beach, surrounded by thick rain forest and coconut plantation, located at a distance of about 11 kms. by jungle land (trek) and 6 kms. by sea. This island is situated at a distance of 85 kms. from Port-Blair, Phoenix Bay Jetty. This island is connected with other places by ferry service. This beach is suitable for snorkeling, diving and swimming but materials should be taken from the Tourism Department, Port Blair.

The Long Island has two guest houses, one is owned by Forest Department and the other by Small Scale Unit. Tourists can stay in the Forest Guest House with the prior permission from the Forest Department, Haddo. Tourists are advised to carry all eatables, essential items from the Long Island shops, as nothing is available on the beach. There are beautiful corals on this beach. Tourists can enjoy the natural scenic beauty from this Jetty. This beach is fast gaining in popularity.

MADHUBAN

Madhuban is situated near Mount Harriet. It is a very beautiful place and a trekking area. This place has a very interesting and a colourful view which is an enchanting and enthralling sight when you see trained elephants carrying out different operations of log extraction in the tropical jungles of these islands. Madhuban is a famous place for taking sea bath. This area also abounds in sunny and golden beaches where one can bask in the sun. Tourists can enjoy the beauty of exotic flora and fauna, endemic birds, animals, butterflies and trained elephants lumbering on. Situated in the North East of South Andaman at a distance of 80 kms. by road from Port Blair Bus Terminus and 25 kms. by sea from Mount Harriet. Tourists go to this place for sun bath and to see the natural beauty of this Madhuban.

MAYABUNDER

It is situated in the northernmost part of Middle Andaman. The distance between Port Blair and Mayabunder is about 240 kms. and Mayabunder and Rangat is about 70 kms. by road. The sea distance between Port Blair and Mayabunder is 135 kms. Mayabunder is the administrative headquarters for the Middle Andaman and North Andaman. The total population of Mayabunder is 23,904, as per the census year 2001 with a growth rate of 10.82% over the census year 1991 (21,570) by getting rural status as per 2001 census. The population of Mayabunder consists mainly of Tamilians, Malayalis, Bengalis and a few Burmese settlers, with a distinct culture. There are 71 census villages in Mayabunder. Mayabunder, being headquarters, has better infrastructural facilities like good hospitals, provision of water, electricity, communications, internal transport etc.

Mayabunder has a number of beaches surrounding it. Of these beaches, a charming beach called Karmatang beach is situated at a distance of 12 kms. from Mayabunder Bus Terminus. Mayabunder has an excellent scenic beauty and, sunrise and sunset are really worth watching. Tourists can reach Mayabunder by road or by boat. The bus journey takes around 7 to 8 hrs. Tourists can enjoy the natural beauty of creeks, mangrove forests, open sea fishes, dances of dolphins, flying fishes etc. while going by boat. While crossing the forest area, the beauty of the forests draws the attention of the tourists. In Mayabunder, there is a beautiful Govt. Guest House under the control of APWD, A&N Administration. Tourists can stay in there by taking prior permission from the Chief Engineer, APWD, Port Blair.

MOUNT HARRIET

This is the second highest peak of these islands (the first one is the Saddle Peak). The height of the Mount Harriet is about 1200 ft. It is situated within 55 kms. by road and 15 kms. by sea from Port Blair. Tourists can reach Mount Harriet in 2 hrs. by road. The sea route is from the Marine Jetty to Hope Town and from there to Mount Harriet by road. This is situated opposite to the Port Blair. After reaching Hope Town by bus or by ferry, it will take another 80 minutes to reach the peak of the Mount Harriet. As per records, the British Chief Commissioners frequently used the Mount Harriet as a summer resort. The Forest Department has constructed a rest house for its own use. However, tourists are also allowed to stay (Indian tourists can stay there overnight) with the permission of the Chief Wildlife Warden, Port Blair/the Forest Department, Haddo. Cauliflower, tomatoes, cabbages, carrots etc. which cannot be grown in Port Blair are planned to be grown here.

Tourists are advised to take eatables, snacks, food and water with them. However, it is said that tea is sold there. All tourists go upto the peak and enjoy the natural scenic beauty. They can see from the peak large parts of South Andaman and other small islands like Havelock, Ross, Neil, etc. and can enjoy rare flora and fauna, endemic birds, animals, butterflies etc. The beautiful scenic view attracts tourists in greater numbers with each day and the crowd is large on Sundays. People enjoy the clouds touching them on the Mount Harriet. At all times the climate is very cool. Hence people go from Port Blair particularly during summer season and stay there for a longer time, i.e. till evening. Even tourists do likewise. So it is named in this book as the "Ooty (a famous tourist place in Tamil Nadu) of the Andaman and Nicobar Islands."

NEIL ISLAND

The Neil Island, commercially, is called as the "Kitchen Garden of the A&N Islands" (Rajavel 1990) since major portion of the consumption of the vegetables in these islands comes from here only. The main work of the people of these islands is vegetable cultivation. The vegetable merchants purchase vegetables at wholesale rates (very cheap rates) and they sell them in the market places at Port Blair, Rangat, Mayabunder, etc. at a very high price. This is a beautiful island with lushgreen forests and sandy beaches. This is an inhabited island covering a total area of 7.3 sq. miles. Mainly Bengalis inhabit this island. Situated at a distance of 45 kms. from Port Blair Phoenix Bay Jetty, the Neil Island has beautiful sand beaches surrounded by the forests which attract tourists. Among the beaches, Sitapur

Beach is the most important one and particularly this beach is surrounded by beautiful tropical rain forests.

Tourists have recently started visiting this beach because of the transport facilities. The A&N Administration operates a ferry service to Neil Island. Normally it takes 4-5 hrs. to reach Neil Island by boat depending upon the weather conditions. The tour operators offer chartered boats but comparatively it turns out very expensive. The Neil Island has one accommodation, run by the Tourism Department where the tourists can stay. The main feature of this island is that the Vegetable wholesalers and agents of from different islands come here to purchase vegetables at cheaper rates and take them to the other islands for selling, particularly in Port Blair. The main feature of this island is its fertile land.

PORT BLAIR CITY

The capital of the territory of Andaman and Nicobar Islands is Port Blair. For the whole territory, this is the only city. Port Blair is the nerve centre of the economy of A&N Islands and hence the development of this city will influence the growth and economic development of other islands and centres. Port Blair city is located in the southeast portion of South Andaman Division. For further details about Port Blair City the chapter 'Historical Fascinations' may be referred.

RANGAT

Economically the place Rangat is getting importance now a days. It is situated in Middle Andaman at a distance of 93 kms. by sea and double this distance by road i.e. 170 kms. from Port Blair. It is the tehsil headquarters and a developing town. It takes 5–6 hrs. to reach Rangat from Port Blair by bus and around 8 hrs. by boat. Rangat has all the infrastructural facilities. The settlers are mainly Tamilians, Malayalis, Bengalis etc.; Rangat is very near Jarawas reserved areas. On inquiry, it is understood that the villages very near to reserved areas are visited by the Jarawas during the night. They steal coconuts, clothes—particularly red coloured, iron items, utensils, bananas etc. The population of Rangat is 38,815 as per the census year 2001 with a growth rate 16.32% over the census year 1991 (33,368) with rural status as per 1991 census.

Vehicle ferries help the transport to cross the two current water creeks namely Middle Strait Jetty and Uttara Jetty. In 6 kms. from Rangat, there is a beautiful beach called Amkunj beach with a total length of about 1½ kms. and width of 40 m. This beach is surrounded by tropical rain forests. One more beach near the Rangat is Chatbut Bay which has a turtle nesting ground. Official tourists who visit Rangat do not go back without seeing this Chatbut Bay beach and the turtles hatching. Tourists can stay in the Guest House owned by the APWD, Port Blair under the control of Executive Engineer, Rangat with the prior permission of the Chief Engineer, Port Blair. A cook is attached with the guest-house. The tourists can have food at a reasonable price. There are private lodges too, where tourists can stay at reasonable tariff. Tourists have to place an order in advance in case of any special items they want, like prawn fry, costly fish like surmai, chicken items etc.

ROSS ISLAND

Once upon a time, the Ross Island had enjoyed the status of Palace Township. During the British period, the Ross Island was the Administrative Headquarters of the Andaman Nicobar Islands. It was developed into self-equipped township with all facilities, required for a civilized colony. Initially, the freedom fighters of the first war of Independence of 1857 brought to Andamans were lodged on the Ross Island. Dr. James Patterson Walker, the Chairman of Andaman committees who arrived in Port Blair on 10th March 1858, established the infamous and the dreaded penal settlement with 200 convicts. British officers lived very happily with all facilities like church, bakery, hospital, bath rooms, swimming pool, tennis ground etc. How the British people (the then) who visited on the postings by the British govt. enjoyed their lives out of the hard physical labour and sufferings of the dedicated Indian Freedom Fighters, Ross islands is the living testimony today for the tourists.

If one thinks seriously about the way Indians were treated by the then merciless British officers, his/her eyes will automatically get moist. This is a secluded island situated in the north of Port Blair harbour and is about 200 acres in area. At present this island is occupied by the Indian Navy. However, it is one of the tourists' attraction places. Tourists can reach this island within 20 minutes from Phoenix Jetty. As far as fascinations are concerned, a small museum named 'Smritika' has been organised and is being maintained by the Indian Navy. This museum depicts the history of the island. Some spotted deer and peacocks are found in this island. All tourists are permitted to visit this precious island but no one is allowed to stay overnight due to security reasons.

SIPPIGHAT

Now a days, the place Sippighat is getting great importance because of divine reasons since, just on the top of the Sippighat bus stand, Sri Ayappa Temple is located. Locals as well as, tourists visit this temple for prayers. This place is situated 14 kms. from Port Blair Bus Terminus on way to Wandoor. Sippighat is very famous for its horticulture farm. The total area of this farm is 80 acres. Scientists contribute their full efforts experimenting many new varieties of plants and species, which have high potential of growth in these islands. As a result of these experiments the excellent growth of clove, pepper, nutmeg, cinnamon, pineapples, papaya, oranges, bananas etc. had been fully justified and it has been proved that they could be propagated on a large scale in these islands. Close to this farm, the Central Agricultural Research Institute has established another experimental farm for growing coconut plants in saline water. Tourists are allowed to go and visit this farm on all working days. Generally tourists going to and coming from Wandoor, Bambooflat, Jirkatang, Ferrargunj etc., will have the privilege of visiting Sippighat since it is situated on way.

VIPER ISLAND

Viper Island is, very near to a famous developing resourceful village called Junglighat. It is visible from the Junglighat Jetty. It situated at a sea distance of 2 kms. from Haddo Jetty and 2 kms. from Junglighat Jetty. It is a separate island. There is no road transport to the island and inside the island. There are many stories about the name of the island i.e. the Viper Island. Some say that this island is named after vipers, with two heads, that were found in plenty in this Island. As vipers are very dangerous that's why this island is named after the snake ostensibly to remind the people not to go to that island. Others say that it is the name of a particular language. But, actually, the island is named as Viper Island in memory of the Vessel called *T S S Viper* in which Lt. Archibald Blair came to these islands from Britain in the year 1876 for the establishment of a penal settlement.

Again, one more reason is that the vessel *T S S Viper* met with an accident and was wrecked near this island. That's why the island is named as Viper Island. As a result of the accident, the British people had chosen this island to keep all prisoners under penal settlement before the construction of Cellular Jail. After the completion of the Cellular Jail, the women prisoners were kept in the Viper Island. The Viper Island Jail had gallows on the top of a hillock. Here in this jail, the condemned women prisoners were hanged. Here the British people used this island to harbour the convicts before the construction of the Cellular Jail. Though the signs of penal settlement are completely obliterated, the jail and its gallows have been retained safely as a tourist spot. Beautiful coconut plantations in the island attract many tourists. Viper Island has a marvellous scenic beauty inside the island as well as from the island.

7

Conclusion

So, fascination in this piece is the economic power of drawing the people towards a place. For any place or places, the most important resources, from the point of view of economic development, are the land resources, favourable location or situation, climate, fertile soil, water resources, fisheries, mineral resources, forest resources, education, socio-cultural resources, historical resources etc. Efficient people develop the country through the capacity of fascinations. As is already explained, the people who go from one place to another place by travel due to various reasons are called Tourists and the whole economic activity related to such travel and tourists is called Tourism which is part of commerce and industry. So, the number of tourists coming to a place to stay fully depends on the power of fascination of the place. The factors and resources responsible for such power of drawing people towards it are known in this work, as Tourism fascinations.

Andaman and Nicobar Islands is blessed with a lot of resources. Such resources are natural resources, forest resources, marine resources, historical resources, socio-cultural resources etc. All such resources have more horse-power of fascination and thereby more number of people of different types, that is, People/Tourists come to these islands for many purposes, namely education and research, to know the history of these islands, to enjoy Nature's beauty, to see the socio-cultural life-style of the people of these islands etc. The Andaman and Nicobar Islands extend its arms and welcomes the tourists of different purposes through its power of fascinations to set up many economic activities for its further growth and development. The tourists are divided into two major classifications, namely Economic Tourists and Non-Economic Tourists. Economic Tourists are those tourists who contribute money for the growth of the economy of these islands. However, the Non-Economic Tourists are those who do not contribute anything to the economy of these islands. The eco-tourism potential of Andaman and Nicobar Islands provides many opportunities for both the protection of the environment and the development of tourism based activities. The Andaman fascinations are classified in the present work, into four types namely—Informational fascinations, Historical fascinations, Social and Cultural fascinations, Educational fascinations and Natural and Places fascinations.

Information is the basis for all kinds of economic activities. Generally, tourists before coming to these far-flung islands, wish to collect particulars and information regarding the places to see, best season to travel and visit, air tickets, ship tickets, fares, accommodation facilities available, tour operators, items to purchase, period of stay, accommodation tariff, procedure to get permission, immigration formalities etc. Any tourist who plans to come to Nature's gifted place like Andaman and Nicobar Islands due to its geographical location would like to have all information to plan for travel. Again, he needs information to take a decision regarding the number of days to stay in Andaman and Nicobar Islands. Whatever be the level of richness in its tourist fascinations, if a destination fails to provide required information on tourism, then tourists will not be attracted and will be dissatisfied. A satisfied tourist is the best advertiser while an unhappy tourist is the worst turndown friend.

After getting information about a particular place, everybody would like to know about the history of the place, its inception, and its population, importance and of all, the speciality of the place. The historical fascinations are the pulling machine affinity of the magnetic inflamed desire about the place. As far as the Andaman and Nicobar Islands is concerned, the tourists are attracted heavily after knowing greater information about the history of these islands. So far in the mainland, the tourists are given a lot of misinformation about the history of these islands. Many times, the author was asked the real history of these islands. The tourists expressed that they were given wrong information about this place, population particularly the tribal population and the climate of these islands. Hence, particulars about the location, history, Cellular Jail, population, including tribals etc. are given in the form of Historical fascinations.

Social and cultural development and tourism development are inter-related. Social and cultural development will attract more tourists and tourism is an important medium of social cultural development. Socio-cultural fascinations are the real tourist fascinations not only for the pleasure point of view but also from education point of view. The Socio–cultural activities are the most important motivating and influencing factors for the tourists to visit these islands. The mixed culture and social life of the people of A&N Islands attract the majority of the tourists who desire to see something new and visualise something different from their own experience. The A&N Islands is a new world, owned by India, having different patterns of life, manners, habits, social traditions, cultural traditions, hospitality, peace, festivals etc., with attractive sites and scenery. Next to the social and cultural activities, fairs and festivals of a particular place plays an important role as they are always associated with joy and happiness. They are the best way of entertaining the people of all age-groups on these occasions when they gather, assemble, exchange their views, work together, worship their gods, etc.

People go from one place to another not only for enjoyment or to spend the holidays, they even go for educational purposes. Educational purpose means the purpose of visiting the place with a view to collect data on the subject-matter of Andaman and Nicobar Islands, to study the situation, activities, growth factor, socio-economic development, to explore the possibility to set up a new venture, to conduct any research work etc. on Andaman and Nicobar Islands. Here there are a lot of areas to attract people on special advantage of educational purposes possessed by each section of the economic section. Tours and travels start to extend its scope to almost all the fields/areas. Again it is the advantage of a particular place to attract the people from various parts of the country and even world due to its speciality. Andaman and Nicobar Islands is the best example of such attractions. This resourceful paradise extends its arms also to scholars from different parts of the mainland to conduct detailed research. Research areas opened for scholars are:

1. Identification of resources
2. Prospects of marine wealth
3. Cost benefit analysis of education, including higher education
4. Prospects of Tourism in Andaman and Nicobar Islands
5. Possibilities of increasing entrepreneurial development
6. Teaching and training for administrators
7. Training Heads of the Institutions
8. Possibilities of developing rural areas
9. Problems of tribals
10. Possibilities of operating air services
11. Possibilities for quality management and administration
12. Possibilities of starting industrial units in rural areas
13. Possibilities of teaching morality to government employees
14. Possibilities of human resource development
15. Possibilities of increasing national income.

Natural fascinations are pollution-free fascinations, which attract the tourists in plenty to these islands. The geology and topography of A&N Islands itself are the most beautiful fascinations. The natural fascinations of these islands are divided into three types namely, Climate, Scenic Beauty and Flora and

Fauna, and the places fascinations are also divided into three types namely Peaceful Places, Ship Journey and Places of Interest.

So in conclusion, I wish to say that the Andaman and Nicobar Islands are a symbol of Peace. Even their location in the remotest part of India adds to their beauty and tranquility. No doubt, it is the solid paradise in green colour on the blue surface. Here, people of different religions from different regions and various states of the country live in harmony. This resourceful territory is free from the so-called poisonous pollutions. Here, in this golden paradise, there is no water or any other kind of pollution. Hence, these islands are the ideal place for people who really want to spend time in pace and joy with their loved ones. Natural scenic beauty, soft cool sea breeze, the beautiful flora and fauna all mesmerise us. Domestic tourists are permitted to visit places at any time without any fear. The people of these islands including the officers and policemen are very helpful to the visitors. Many visitors are said to have become writers after visiting this Green Paradise.

This is a beautiful place for meditation also. Of course, the spots are to be developed. As during vacations people go to a hill station to spend their holidays, they can visit this place. By knowing the right time and season to visit, they can come to the paradise and enjoy the brimming beauty of these islands. But majority of tourists have very little information about the seasons of this Green Paradise. The tables given in the chapters will give you the information about the position of the season. This information has been collected personally out of the practical experiences in the last three years. The scenic beauty of the islands emerges like a beautiful green oasis in the Bay of Bengal. A most hospitable and cosmopolitan society, free from rigidity of caste, creed and religion, projecting Indian culture, unity in diversity is the A&N Islands, today. The undulating terrain, the inter-play of land, sea and creeks, the bright white trips of sea beaches that is, the blue bays, the rich tropical forests fringed by bright green mangroves, all combine to enhance the scenic value of these Islands in a way not to be found anywhere else in the country. So, if one comes to these islands to enjoy the peacefulness of this place, certainly he will go back with a high level of satisfaction.

No doubt, there may be some problems in developing tourism in these islands. But for every problem, there are solutions with merits and demerits. If the solutions are cautiously selected through meaningful discussions, consultations with the qualified persons and researchers, and if the selected solutions are carefully constructed in the form of policies, procedures, programmes, rules and strategies and if they are rightly implemented by the dedicated and sincere personnel, then all the fascinations mentioned in this piece of work will have more meaning and strength of power to allure charmingly, captivatingly, and with a high level of aesthetics.

Bibliography

1. AMBASHT, N. K., 1970. *Critical Study of Tribal Education.* New Delhi: S. Chand & Co.

2. BASU, B.K., 1990. *The Onge Negrito Hunter-gatherers of Little Andaman.* Kolkata: Seagull Books.

3. BROWN RADCLIFF, A.R., 1922. *The Andaman Islanders.* London: Weidenfeld & Nicolson.

4. CHAK, B.L., 1967. *Andaman and Nicobar Islands,* Ministry of Information and Broadcasting. New Delhi: Government of India.

5. CIPRIANI, L., 1966. *The Andaman Islanders.* London: Weidenfeld & Nicolson.

6. DAS, S.T., 1982. *The Andaman and Nicobar Islands.* New Delhi: Sagar Publishers.

7. GUPTA, B., 1976. *Andaman: The Land of Primitives.* Kolkata: Jinjnasa Publications.

8. JUSTIN, A., 1990. *The Nicobarese.* Kolkata: Anthropological Survey of India.

9. KLOSS, C.B., 1903. *In the Andaman and Nicobar Islands.* London: John Murray (Indian reprint 1971).

10. MAN, E. H., 1883. *The Aboriginal Inhabitants of Andaman Islands.* London: Indian reprint Delhi, Sanskaran Prakasan.

11. MATHUR, K.K., 1967. *Nicobar Islands.* Delhi: Sterling Publishers (p) Ltd.

12. PANDIT, T.N., 1990. *The Sentinalese.* Anthropological Survey of India, Calcutta.

13. PORTMAN, M. V., 1899. *A History of our relations with Andamanese.* Kolkata: Superintendent of Govt. Printing Press.

14. RAJAVEL, N., 1998. *Tourism in Andaman and Nicobar Islands.* Delhi: Manas Publications.

15. RAJAVEL, N., 2003. *Management of Higher Educational Institutions,* Delhi: New Century Publications.

16. RICHARDSON, REV. C. H., 1947. *The Car Nicobar under Japanese Occupation 1943-45* (Car Nicobar).

17. RIZVI, S.N.H., 1990. *The Shompen: A Vanishing Tribe of the Great Nicobar Island.* Kolkata: Seagull Books.

18. SALDANHA, C.J. 1989. *Andaman Nicobar and Lakshwadeep, an Environment Impact Assessment.* New Delhi: Oxford and IBH Publishing Co, Pvt. Ltd.

19. SARKAR, S.S., 1951. *The Aboriginal Races of India.* Kolkata: Bookland Private Ltd.

20. SARKAR. J. 1990. *The Jarawa.* Kolkata: Seagull Books.

21. SEN. P. K., 1964. *Land and People of the Andamans.* Kolkata: Post Graduate Mart

22. SPLINDER, GEORGE D., 1963. (Ed) *Education and Culture.* New York: Rinehart and Winston Inc.

23. TAMTA, B.R., 1992. *Andaman and Nicobar Islands.* New Delhi: National Book Trust:

24. VAIDYA, SURESH. 1960. *Islands of Mary Gold Sun.* Delhi: Hindi Pocket Books (p) Ltd.

25. WHITEHEAD, GEORGE. 1924. *In the Nicobar Islands.* London: Seeley Services & Co., Ltd:

Index